Love and Sex After 60

Also by Robert N. Butler, M.D.,
and Myrna I. Lewis, A.C.S.W.

Aging and Mental Health: Positive Psychosocial and Biomedical Approaches (Third Edition)

Midlife Love Life: How to Deal with the Physical and Emotional Changes of Midlife and Their Effect on Your Sex Life

Also by Robert N. Butler, M.D.

Why Survive? Being Old in America

Human Aging (co-author)

Love and Sex After 60

Revised Edition

Robert N. Butler, M.D., and Myrna I. Lewis, A.C.S.W.

Harper & Row, Publishers, New York

Cambridge, Philadelphia, San Francisco, London
Mexico City, São Paulo, Singapore, Sydney

Grateful acknowledgment is made for permission to reprint:

Tables from *The Essential Guide to Prescription Drugs* (fourth edition) and *The Essential Guide to Prescription Drugs 1988* by James W. Long, M.D. Reprinted with permission of Harper & Row, Publishers, Inc. Copyright 1985, 1988.

Table from *The New Our Bodies, Ourselves* by The Boston Women's Health Book Collective. Reprinted with permission of Simon & Schuster, Inc. Copyright © 1984 by The Boston Women's Health Book Collective, Inc.

Tables from "Many Common Medications Can Affect Sexual Expression" by James W. Long, M.D. Reprinted with permission from *Generations,* 833 Market Street, Suite 516, San Francisco, CA 94103. Copyright 1981, WGS, ASA.

Designed by Joan Greenfield

Library of Congress Cataloging-in-Publication Data

Butler, Robert N., 1927–
  Love and sex after 60.

  Rev. ed. of: Sex after sixty. 1st ed. c1976.
  Bibliography: p.
  Includes index.
  1. Sex instruction for the aged. 2. Aged—Psychology.
3. Sex (Psychology). 4. Love. I. Lewis, Myrna I.
II. Butler, Robert N., 1927–   . Sex after sixty.
III. Title. IV. Title: Love and sex after sixty.
HQ55.B87   1988   613.9′6   87-46124
ISBN 0-06-055125-9   88 89 90 91 92 DT/FG 10 9 8 7 6 5 4 3 2 1
ISBN 0-06-096270-4 (pbk.) 88 89 90 91 92 DT/FG 10 9 8 7 6 5 4 3 2 1

Contents

PREFACE   ix

1. *Sex After Sixty*   1

2. *Normal Physical Changes in Sex and
   Sexuality With Age*   8

3. *Common Medical Problems and Sex*   29

4. *The Sexual Effects of Drugs (Including Alcohol)
   and Surgery*   60

5. *Sexual Fitness*   81

6. *Common Emotional Problems With Sex*   98

7. *People Without Partners:
   Finding New Relationships*   116

8. *Learning New Patterns of Lovemaking*   131

9. *Dating, Remarriage, and Your Children*   140

10. *Where to Go for Help*   148

11. *The Second Language of Sex*   159

    GLOSSARY   167

    BIBLIOGRAPHY   175

    INDEX   177

Preface

This revision resulted from a curious dilemma. The first edition of *Love and Sex After 60* was published in 1976. Ten years later we wrote a greatly expanded revision, essentially a new book, called *Midlife Love Life*. It was designed not only to update the information on sexuality for older people, but to include the middle-aged as well. Our reasoning was that middle age is the ideal time to begin paying attention to what promotes good functioning throughout the last half of the life cycle. To our surprise, a number of our older readers objected, feeling they deserved their own book, particularly since so little literature on this subject exists exclusively for them. We sat down to revise again, and with this new edition, sans the middle-aged, we hope to have worked ourselves out of this dilemma. Both books, *Midlife Love Life* and *Love and Sex After 60,* are now in print. Both contain updated information—but the former includes the middle-aged, while the latter concentrates solely on older people.

Our aim is to bring to older people the latest on the dynamic subject of sexuality. There is much that is new and heartening. There are still negative stereotypes to challenge. And there is much that is continuing to evolve in the understanding of the physical and psychological issues of later-life sexuality. The diagnosis and treatment of sexual problems has greatly improved since the mid-1970s. The public, the professions, and older people themselves have become more aware of the importance of sexuality as one grows older and more comfortable with the subject. And we humans seem to be slowly maturing in our capacity to recognize that the added gift of life, an average of twenty-five more years of life expectancy since the turn of the century, is giving us an unprecedented opportunity to develop the art of living more richly and fully.

Love and Sex After 60

Chapter 1

Sex After Sixty

O ur society is in the midst of a longevity revolution resulting from a gain of twenty-five years of average life
expectancy in the past eighty-five years. Every day
6,000 Americans turn sixty. Altogether forty million people, or
one out of every six of us, is sixty or older. What happens to
sexuality at this time of life? Many people—not only the young
and middle-aged but older people themselves—simply assume
that it is over. This is nonsense. Our own clinical and research
work, the work of other gerontologists, the research of Kinsey,
and the clinical discoveries of Masters and Johnson all demonstrate that relatively healthy older people who enjoy sex are
capable of experiencing it—often until *very* late in life. Those who
do have sexual problems can frequently be helped.

We have written this book for those older men and women
who are presently or potentially interested in sexuality and would
like to know more about what is likely to happen to their sexuality
over time. We will offer solutions to sexual problems that may
occur and propose means for countering negative attitudes that
older people may experience—within themselves, from family
members, from the medical and psychotherapeutic professions,
and from society at large. We especially want older people to
know that their concerns and problems are not unique, that they
are not alone in their experience, and that many others feel
exactly as they do. Even those people who have had a lively

1

enthusiasm and capacity for sex all their lives often need information, support, and sometimes various kinds of treatment in order to continue sexual activity as the years go by. In addition, people for whom sex may not have been especially satisfying in their younger days may find that it is possible to improve its quality despite long-standing difficulties.

Sex and sexuality are pleasurable, rewarding, and fulfilling experiences that enhance the later years. They are also—as everyone knows—enormously complex psychologically. Every one of us carries with us throughout our lives a weight of infant and childhood experiences related to sex that have been shaped by ourselves, our parents, our families, our teachers, and our society, some of which are positive and some negative, some of which we realize and many of which we are unaware.

Because of this, it is useful to understand what underlies so many of the attitudes and problems about sex that one encounters. If you are an older person, be prepared for the likelihood of conflicting feelings within yourself and contradictory attitudes from the outside world. Should older people have sex lives? Are they able to make love? Do they really want to? Is it appropriate —that is, "normal" or "decent"—or is sexual interest a sign of "senility" and brain disease (he/she has gone "daft"), poor judgment, or an embarrassing inability to adjust to aging with proper restraint and resignation?

How much less troubling it would be to accept the folklore of cookie-baking grandmothers who bustle about the kitchen making goodies for their loved ones while rocking-chair grandfathers puff on their pipes and reminisce. Idealized folk figures like these are not supposed to have sex lives of their own. After all, they are our parents and grandparents, not ordinary adults with the same needs and desires that we have.

As an older man or woman, you may find that love and sex in later life, when they are acknowledged at all, will be patronizingly thought of as "cute" or "sweet," like the puppy love of teenagers; but even more likely, they will be ridiculed, a subject for jokes that have undercurrents of disdain and apprehensiveness

2

at the prospect of growing older. Our language is full of telltale phrases: older men become "dirty old men," "old fools," or "old goats" where sex is involved. Older women are depicted as "biddies" and "hags." Most of this "humor" implies the impotence of older men and the ugliness of older women.

A mythology fed by misinformation surrounds late-life sexuality. The presumption is that sexual desire automatically ebbs with age—that it begins to decline when one is in one's forties, proceeds relentlessly downward (you are "losing it"), and eventually hits bottom (you are "over the hill") at some time between sixty and sixty-five. Thus an older woman who shows an evident, perhaps even a lusty, interest in sex is often assumed to be suffering from "emotional" problems; and if she is obviously in her right mind and sexually active, she runs the risk of being called "depraved" or, more kindly, said to be clinging pathetically to her lost youth.

Lustiness in young men is often seen as lechery in older men. Even simple affection can be misunderstood. An older man's show of warmth toward children other than his own grandchildren or those of his friends runs the risk of an assumption that it is sexually tinged. "Child molesting," popularly associated with older men, is actually a crime committed primarily by young men in their twenties.

From time to time everybody is caught up by accounts of older people who perform sexual feats "despite" their age. Newspapers relish them: "92-year-old-man is father of twins"; "Woman of 73 and man of 76 arrested by police in love nest"; "Judge of 81 marries 22-year-old showgirl"; "72-year-old woman jailed for attempted prostitution." In the popular mind these older people walk the thin line between sexual heroics and indecency, with part of the public saying "More power to them" and the remainder reacting with disgust. Everyone, however, reads the accounts with the mixture of revulsion and fascination reserved for the extraordinary and the bizarre.

Why are we so negative about sex in later life and about older people in general? Much of this attitude, of course, is an outgrowth of our own fear of growing old and dying, and it has given rise to a prejudice we have called *ageism,* which is systematic discrimination against people because they are old, just as racism and sexism discriminate for reasons of skin color and gender. The ageist sees older people in stereotypes: rigid, boringly talkative, senile, old-fashioned in morality and lacking in skills, useless and with little redeeming social value. There's a fine irony in the fact that if the ageists live long enough they are going to end up being "old" themselves and the victims, in turn, of their own prejudice. When this realization penetrates, these attitudes can turn into self-hatred. A great many older people have fallen into this trap, often at devastating cost to their personal happiness. As far as sexuality is concerned, ageism is largely a matter of desexualization in its ultimate form; if you are getting old, you're finished.

Some of these attitudes have roots in memories of a relatively recent past. At the turn of the century, when the average life expectancy was forty-seven years, few older people lived to old age and fewer still were healthy enough to be sexually active. But today life expectancy is seventy-four years and we have a large population of relatively healthy people over sixty-five. Of these, 95 percent live in the community, 81 percent can get around by themselves, and about 30 percent are still working part- or full-time. (We now term the age period sixty-five to seventy-four "early old age" and call that over seventy-five "later old age.") We have not accepted these new realities, however, nor have popular attitudes caught up; the general image of late life still assumes frailty or decrepitude.

If we join these cultural attitudes with the prevalent sexual "yardsticks" by which we are all influenced, it is no wonder that older people may be confused and uncertain about sex. Both men and women worry about "wearing out" physically. They want to know what changes are to be expected with normal aging, whether there is reasonable hope for a physically healthy and active sex life, and whether sex can be as good as it was when they were younger.

Men are special victims of a lifelong excessive emphasis on physical performance. Masculinity is equated with physical prowess. Older men judge themselves and are judged by comparing the frequency and potency of their sexual performance with that of younger men. These comparisons seldom place any value on experience and on the quality of sex. When measured by standards that are essentially athletic, older men are naturally considered inferior. They often panic at the first sign of change: "Lately I've been troubled by the fact that I seem to take longer to have a good erection. Is something wrong? Am I becoming impotent? Will I be able to have a firm erection as I get older? Will sex be as pleasurable as when I was younger? Will my partner think I am inadequate?"

Women are under less pressure in terms of performance, of course, but they, too, worry about changes. They may report they are losing their "grip," namely the muscle strength in the vagina that enables them to hold a penis. The size of the vagina itself may change, and there may be problems with "dryness" as vaginal lubrication lessens. Some women begin to experience pain during intercourse and want to know what to do to eliminate it.

But the predominant pressure on women comes from what can be termed "aesthetic narrowness," that widespread assumption that only the young are beautiful. Many older people believe this themselves. When women's hair turns gray, and their skins develop wrinkles, and their bodies lose their earlier firmness and suppleness, they are very likely to see themselves as unattractive. The idea of beauty needs a more sophisticated definition that includes character, intelligence, expressiveness, knowledge, achievement, disposition, tone of voice and speech patterns, posture and bearing, warmth, personal style, social skills —all those personal traits that make each individual unique and that can be found at any age.

In late life we find just as many complaints between partners about sexual incompatibilities as at any other time: interest on one side and disinterest on the other, or passivity, or rebuffs, or failure to agree on frequency. Problems also arise between couples when one partner is incapacitated or chronically ill and the other is healthy. If the healthy partner has active sexual needs, anger and irritation often lead to guilt, as if one were lacking the appropriate concern and compassion for the ailing partner. The latter, in turn, may feel guilty at being unable to participate in lovemaking.

Tension in the later years often arises when those who are parents are inhibited by sons and daughters who find it uncomfortable to accept sexuality in their mothers and fathers. (We all know that, God forbid, *our* parents were not interested in sex!) Many adults continue to be bound by a primitive childhood need to deny their parents a sex life and to lock them into purely parental roles. For these children their parents are never fellow adults. Nor are the motivations always psychological. Avarice and selfishness are, unhappily, common. If one parent dies, children may try to prevent the surviving parent from meeting new friends (and potential new partners) in order to protect their inheritance. Any evidence of parental sexuality or romance threatens them.

We have been sketching a number of ways—positive and negative—in which individuals and society react to sex in older people. But what if you are not particularly interested in sex? Sizable numbers of older people feel this way. We want to emphasize that sexual disinterest is a matter of concern only if you find it personally troubling or if it causes problems in relating to others. Certain older people never were significantly interested in sex even as young people, whether because of biological makeup or, more often, as a result of social conditioning. For others sex has been a long-standing focus of emotional conflict resulting from or causing difficult relations with their partners. For them and their partners the opportunity to discontinue sex under the socially acceptable guise of "sexless old age" can be a great relief.

There are others who have simply grown tired of sex. It may have been shared with the same partner routinely for many years, and they have compensated for its dullness by developing satisfying nonsexual activities. Other people may have stopped sex because of disabilities or serious illnesses. When their health improved there was often no motivation to change what had become a comfortable habit. Sometimes an individual will have made a deliberate decision to share sex only with a particular partner, and when illness or death intervened, sex ended. Other people view sex only for procreation, not pleasure, and feel their religion supports this conviction, so sex ends with the completion of the menopause. Self-imposed abstinence from sex may also be the continuation of a lifelong habit. This can often be traced back to frightening early experiences or to feelings that sex is forbidden and dangerous, and the avoidance of sex altogether may provide an adjustment that works reasonably well.

Whatever the reasons, it is possible to live a happy and satisfying life without sex if that is one's choice, and a good many older people do exactly that. American public attention and emphasis on sexuality has had the effect of making many of the young and middle-aged feel guilty, inadequate, or incomplete if sex fails to play a central role in their lives, and we do not want to place a similar burden on older people. Those who have neither a desire for nor an interest in sex, or who have deliberately chosen a life-style in which sexuality plays little or no part, are entitled to live the life they find most fulfilling.

On the other hand, those older people who do enjoy sex deserve encouragement and support, as well as necessary information and appropriate treatment if problems arise. Sexuality, the physical and emotional responsiveness to sexual stimuli, goes beyond the sex urge and the sex act. For many older people it offers the opportunity to express not only passion but affection, esteem, and loyalty. It provides affirmative evidence that one can count on one's body and its functioning. It allows people to assert themselves positively. It carries with it the possibility of excitement and romance. It expresses delight in being alive. It offers a continuous challenge to grow and change in new directions.

Chapter 2

Normal Physical Changes in Sex and Sexuality With Age

What happens to your body sexually as it ages? There are significant changes in the physical and physiological aspects of sex with age, but in the absence of disease or adverse drug effects, such changes do not usually cause sexual problems.

The act of sex is complex, encompassing the body, the mind, and the emotions. It involves the nervous system and the hormones as well as specific organs of the body. All participate in the sexual-response cycle, which includes sexual desire, followed by excitement or erotic arousal, orgasm or climax, and resolution or recovery. Both men and women experience similar sexual responses.

People are stimulated sexually in a number of ways—through sight, smell, touch, thoughts, and feelings. The pelvic area reacts. Muscle tension and congestion (filling of the blood vessels) occur, especially in the sexual or genital organs. The sex hormones that play an active role in this responsiveness are steroids, produced in the adrenal glands of both men and women and in the ovaries of women and the testes of men. Estrogen, one of the active female hormones, has a profound effect on the development and functioning of the female sex organs. Androgen, the primary male hormone, appears to influence sexual desire in both men and women (women have small amounts of androgen) as well as sexual development and performance in men. Hormone levels are influenced by the body's master gland, the pituitary, in the brain.

Older Women

Most of the sexual changes in women can be directly traced to the decline of female hormones, especially estrogen, associated with the menopause. Menopause, also called the "change of life" or "climacteric," is a physiological process that continues for several years and takes place anywhere between the ages of thirty-five and fifty-five but usually between forty-five and fifty. It involves fluctuations in estrogen levels from previously normal levels (prior to menopause) to near zero. Its most conspicuous sign is the cessation of menstruation.

The menopause is a rich source of folklore about insanity, the loss of sexual desire and attractiveness, the inevitability of depression, the occurrence of severe physical symptoms, and masculinization. Actually, 60 percent of all women experience no remarkable physical or emotional symptoms with menopause, and most of those who do, experience only minimal to moderate physical problems. Symptoms resulting from hormonal imbalance may include hot flashes, headaches and neckaches, excessive fatigue, and feelings of emotional instability. None of these are inevitable, and when they do occur, they often can be greatly alleviated or sometimes entirely relieved by various treatments. Life stresses can precipitate or exacerbate menopausal symptoms, and psychological counseling can be helpful under those circumstances. Even left untreated, certain menopausal symptoms subside spontaneously in time.

During or, more usually, following menopause, large numbers of older women begin to show signs of estrogen or sex-steroid deprivation, which can affect their sexual functioning. Many women complain of a feeling of "dryness" or "loss of juices" in the vagina, particularly during sexual intercourse. Vaginal lubrication produced by congestion of the blood vessels in the vaginal wall is the physiological equivalent of erection in the man. Lubrication of the walls of the vagina begins to take longer as a woman grows older. This seems to be due both to the loss of estrogen necessary to produce the secretions and to changes in the structure of the vaginal wall itself, through which the secretions ooze. When this happens, intercourse may feel scratchy, rough, and eventually painful.

Typically, the lining of the vagina begins to thin and become easily irritated, leading to pain and sometimes to cracking and bleeding during and after intercourse. The vagina can no longer as easily absorb the shock of a thrusting penis. Such pain (dyspareunia) occurs especially if intercourse is of long duration or following a long period without sexual contact. Sometimes the shape of the vagina itself changes, becoming narrower, shorter, and less elastic, although it generally continues to be more than large enough for intercourse. Estrogen replacement therapy has been used for protection against vaginal atrophy and dryness. However, since it has been associated with a somewhat increased risk of endometrial, or uterine, cancer and certain other problems, women and their doctors may be anxious about the risks of this kind of remedy. (See pages 13–20 for a more detailed discussion of estrogen replacement therapy.)

Pain and discomfort of any kind in the vaginal area should be taken seriously by women and their physicians since pain obviously interferes with sexual pleasure and response. In many cases, but not always, physicians can tell during a vaginal exam whether a woman has vaginal atrophy severe enough to cause pain. Other causes of pain are endometriosis, a fixed retroverted uterus, a prolapsed ovary, or water in the Fallopian tubes (hydrosalpinx)—all of which need medical attention.

With loss of estrogen the usually acid vaginal secretions become less acidic, increasing the possibility of vaginal infection and causing burning, itching, and discharge. This condition is variously called estrogen-deficient, steroid-deficient, atrophic, or "senile" vaginitis. If infection is untreated and spreads to the bladder, it produces an inflammation called cystitis. These conditions are curable, and they should be treated by a doctor. Home douching should not be attempted unless your doctor instructs you to do so, because it can confuse the diagnosis and may not, in any case, be the recommended treatment.

Do not assume that all vaginal itching and discharge reflect estrogen deficiency. There should be a complete examination, including a Pap test, to rule out the possibility of a tumor of the reproductive tract. Allergies, trichomoniasis, and yeast and fungus infections (especially in diabetics) are other causes of itching; womb prolapse (fallen womb) may produce a vaginal discharge.

With the thinning of the vaginal walls, the bladder and urethra (the tube through which the urine is passed) are less protected and may be irritated during intercourse. Older women can develop what is sometimes called "honeymoon cystitis," an inflammation of the bladder resulting from bruising and jostling. This tends to be an irritative condition initially, rather than a bacterial infection. When bacteria are present, however, it becomes a fullfledged cystitis, characterized by an unrelenting, irresistible urge to urinate, accompanied by a burning sensation, and must be treated medically. Advanced stages bring an increasingly painful burning during urination, waking at night to urinate, and, occasionally, blood in the urine. Suggestions for preventing and treating urinary tract infections are included under "Home Remedies" on pages 21–23.

The clitoris may be slightly reduced in size very late in life, although this is not always the case. The lips of the vagina (the labia) may become less firm. The covering of the clitoris and the fat pad in the hair-covered pubic area lose some of their fatty tissue, leaving the clitoris less protected and more easily irritated. However, it still remains the source of intense sexual sensation and orgasm, essentially as it was in earlier years.

Women in good health who were able to have orgasms in their younger years can continue having orgasms until very late in life, well into their eighties. (Indeed, some women begin to have orgasms for the first time as they grow older. Lack of orgasmic ability earlier in life does not necessarily mean that such a pattern will continue.) It is unclear whether the length of time required to reach orgasm changes with age in women. Nor do we know for certain whether there are changes in the duration and intensity of an orgasm with age. Shorter-lasting orgasms and spasms in the uterus, when they occur, may be evidence of hormonal imbalance.

Except for the effects of estrogen loss after menopause, the normal physical changes that accompany aging interfere little with female sexual ability. Reports of a decline in women's sexual interest as they age seem to be predominantly psychologically defensive or protective in origin rather than physiological. The actual frequency of sexual intercourse in women tends to be more affected by their partners' age, health, and level of sexual interest and functioning than a reflection of reduced interest or capacity in women themselves.

Treatment of Postmenopausal Changes

Regular Sexual Activity. Although still controversial, there is some evidence that regular sexual activity helps preserve functioning, especially lubricatory ability, and may even stimulate estrogen production. Sexually active women also seem to have less vaginal atrophy. The regular muscle contractions during sexual activity and orgasm do maintain vaginal muscle tone, and it is thought that intercourse helps preserve the shape and size of the vaginal space.

Following the death or illness of a partner, many women find themselves without the opportunity for sexual contact. If it is psychologically acceptable, self-stimulation (masturbation) can be effective in preserving lubricating ability and the muscle tone that maintains the size and shape of the vagina. In addition, it can release tension, stimulate sexual appetite, and contribute to general well-being. Self-stimulation is probably more common among younger women because they have grown up in a less restrictive sexual atmosphere. But it seems clear that it is being practiced by women of all ages with growing frequency, lessened anxiety, and considerable physical benefit. In fact, self-stimulation is in-

Possible Contraindications to the Use of Estrogen Replacement Therapy (ERT) Postmenopausally

This drug should not be taken if

you have had a significant allergic reaction to any dosage form of it previously.

you have a history of thrombophlebitis, embolism, heart attack or stroke.

you have seriously impaired liver function.

you have abnormal and unexplained vaginal bleeding.

you have sickle cell disease.

Inform your physician before taking this drug if

you have had an unfavorable reaction to estrogen therapy previously.

you have a history of cancer of the breast or reproductive organs.

you have any of the following conditions: fibrocystic breast changes, fibroid tumors of the uterus, endometriosis, migrainelike headaches, epilepsy, asthma, heart disease, high blood pressure, gallbladder disease, diabetes or porphyria.

you smoke tobacco on a regular basis.

you plan to have surgery in the near future.

Reprinted from The Essential Guide to Prescription Drugs 1988 *by James W. Long, M.D. (Harper & Row, 1988).*

creasingly viewed not only as a response to loss of sexual contact with a partner but also as a natural and ongoing supplementary activity within a relationship.

Hormone Replacement Therapy. Throughout the 1960s and until the mid-1970s, estrogen in its most popular form, Premarin, was liberally prescribed by physicians for treatment of the discomforts of menopause. Estrogen was promoted as a protection against hot flashes, vaginal atrophy, heart disease, depression, lowered sex drive, osteoporosis, cancer, general aging signs like wrinkles and gray hair, and breast cancer. Common side effects were thought to be occasional dose-related uterine bleeding and

Considerations in the Use of Estrogens for Treating the Menopausal Syndrome

Possible benefits	Possible risks
Effective relief of menopausal hot flushes and night sweats	Increased risk of cancer of the uterus with 3+ years of continual use
Prevention or relief of atrophic vaginitis, atrophy of the vulva and urethra	Increased frequency of gallstones
Prevention of osteoporosis	Accelerated growth of preexisting fibroid tumors of the uterus
Prevention of thinning of the skin	
Mental tonic effect	Fluid retention
	Postmenopausal bleeding
	Deep vein thrombophlebitis and thromboembolism (less likely with conjugated estrogens, more likely with synthetic unconjugated hormones)
	Increased blood pressure (rare)
	Decreased sugar tolerance (rare)

General principles for the use of estrogen in treating estrogen-deficiency states

It is now generally held that for the well-informed menopausal woman who has obvious symptoms of estrogen deficiency and does not have any contraindications to its use, the benefits of estrogen replacement therapy outweigh the possible risks. The use of estrogen is considered effective and safe when prescribed appropriately and monitored properly.

As each woman reaches the menopausal years (45 to 55), she should assess her own status and perceived needs. Next she should familiarize herself with the benefits and possible risks of estrogen replacement therapy. If she thinks she needs medical guidance and/or treatment, she should discuss all aspects of her situation with her physician and share in the decision regarding the use of hormones.

A clear indication for the use of estrogen should exist. It should not be given routinely to the menopausal woman, but should be reserved to treat those with symptoms of estrogen deficiency. Estrogen does not retard the natural progression of general aging; it should not be used for the sole purpose of "preserving femininity."

Before estrogen therapy is started, appropriate examinations should be performed and due consideration given to the following possible contraindications to the use of estrogen:

1. Pregnancy
2. History of deep venous thrombosis or pulmonary embolism
3. Present or previous cancer of the breast
4. Cancer of the uterus
5. Strong family history of breast or uterine cancer
6. Current liver disease or previous drug-induced jaundice
7. Chronic gallbladder disease, with or without stones
8. Abnormal elevation of blood fats (cholesterol, triglycerides, etc.)
9. History of porphyria
10. Large uterine fibroid tumors
11. Any estrogen-dependent tumor
12. Combination of obesity, varicose veins and cigarette smoking
13. Diabetes mellitus
14. Severe hypertension

In the young woman experiencing premature menopause (destruction or removal of both ovaries), the *long-term* use of estrogen replacement is justified, provided appropriate precautions are observed (see Guidelines, pages 17–20).

In the menopausal woman experiencing hot flushes and/or atrophic vaginitis, the *short-term* use of estrogen therapy is generally felt to be acceptable with appropriate supervision and guidance. Estrogen replacement therapy provides symptomatic relief; it is not a permanent cure for hot flushes.

Long-term estrogen therapy for *all* women after the menopause cannot be justified. Treatment must be carefully individualized (see Guidelines, pages 17–20).

It is generally recommended that estrogens be taken cyclically. The customary schedule is from the 1st through the 25th day of each month, with no estrogen during the remaining days of the month. After 6 to 12 months of continuous use, the estrogen dose should be gradually reduced over a period of 2 to 3 months and then discontinued to assess the individual's need for resumption of use.

(continued)

15

The lowest effective daily dose of estrogen should be determined and maintained for the duration of the treatment.

Vaginal cream preparations of estrogen may be considered instead of orally administered estrogen if the only indication is atrophic vaginitis. However, it should be noted that these preparations allow rapid absorption of estrogen into the systemic circulation, and do not permit accurate control of dosage. They should be used intermittently and only as needed to correct the symptoms of atrophic vaginitis. (Note: The estrogen in vaginal creams can be absorbed through the skin of the penis and cause tenderness of the breast in men.)

The unnecessary prolongation of estrogen therapy should be avoided. It is advisable to use estrogens in the lowest effective dose and for only as long as necessary to relieve symptoms.

Reprinted from The Essential Guide to Prescription Drugs 1988 *by James W. Long, M.D. (Harper & Row, 1988).*

minor complaints of nausea, fluid retention, weight gain, and increased susceptibility to vaginal yeast infection.

The use of menopausal hormones declined sharply for a number of years after five studies in 1975–76 definitely showed that estrogen replacement therapy (ERT) was associated with an increased risk of endometrial cancer, especially if estrogen was taken for more than one year. Currently doctors are once again prescribing ERT thanks to new guidelines for use that include smaller and shorter-term dosages, often combined with another female hormone, progestin, and a greater clarity about contraindications. However, estrogen replacement therapy is still controversial. For circumstances under which estrogen should not be used at all or should be used with caution, see the table on page 13. A listing of possible benefits and risks has been provided in the table on page 14.

If ERT is used, medical consensus holds that the lowest effective dose for the shortest possible period of time is desirable, unless the purpose of therapy is the prevention or treatment of osteoporosis, which requires a larger dosage (see the table on pages 17–19). If estrogen is being used long-term for vaginal atro-

Guidelines for the Use of Estrogens in Specific
Deficiency States

---

*I. The woman experiencing the "menopausal syndrome" of hot flushes
and sweating (usually 45 to 55 years of age):*

A. Uterus not removed
  1. Choice of hormones and recommended dosage range:
      Estrogen: conjugated equine estrogens—0.3 to 0.625 mg
        daily. (See list of alternative estrogen preparations, page
        20).
      Progestin: medroxyprogesterone—5 to 10 mg daily.
      The lowest effective dose of estrogen should be used.*
  2. Dosage schedule:
      Estrogen: once daily from the 1st through the 25th day of each
        month.
      Progestin: once daily during the last 7 to 10 days of the
        estrogen course.†
  3. Duration of use: 6 to 12 months, followed by gradual reduction
      of dose over a period of 2 to 3 months, and then
      discontinuation to assess the need for continued use.
      Treatment should be resumed only if symptoms require it. An
      attempt should be made to discontinue all hormones after 2 to
      3 years of continual use, unless a clear need for continuation is
      apparent.
  4. Periodic examinations:
      Base-line mammogram (low-radiation-dose xeroradiography).
      Low-dose mammogram annually (over 50 years of age) during
        continuous use of estrogen (American Cancer Society
        guideline).
      Self-examination of breasts monthly.

(continued)

---

  * The lowest effective dose is determined by keeping a daily "flush
count" to ascertain the lowest daily dose that will reduce the frequency
and severity of flushes to an acceptable level.
  † The use of a supplemental progestin during the last 7 to 10 days
of estrogen administration is still controversial. A possible benefit is
the reduced potential for uterine cancer; a possible risk is the increased
potential for coronary artery disease; a possible inconvenience is withdrawal bleeding (induced menstruation). The risks of this form of long-
term progestin therapy are not known.

Physican examination of breasts every 6 to 12 months.
Cervical cytology and endometrial biopsy (aspiration curettage)
annually..
Blood pressure measurement every 3 to 6 months.
Two-hour blood sugar assay annually.

B. Uterus removed

1. Choice of estrogen and dose: conjugated equine estrogens—
0.3 to 0.625 mg daily.
The lowest effective dose should be used.*

2. Dosage schedule: once daily from the 1st through the 25th day
of each month.

3. Duration of use: 6 to 12 months, followed by gradual reduction
of dose over a period of 2 to 3 months, and then
discontinuation to assess the need for continued use.
Treatment should be resumed only if symptoms require it. An
attempt should be made to discontinue all hormones after 2 to
3 years of continual use.

4. Periodic examinations:
Base-line mammogram (low-radiation-dose xeroradiography).
Low-dose mammogram annually (over 50 years of age) during
continuous use of estrogen (American Cancer Society
guideline).
Self-examination of breasts monthly.
Physician examination of breasts every 6 to 12 months.
Blood pressure measurement every 3 to 6 months.
Two-hour blood sugar assay annually.

---

*II. The woman in the "post-menopausal" period (usually over 55 years
of age): treatment should be individualized as follows:*

---

1. If there are no specific symptoms of estrogen deficiency (hot
flushes or atrophic vaginitis), estrogen should not be given.

2. If specific symptoms of estrogen deficiency persist to a degree
requiring subjective relief, the recommendations in Part I above
apply. However, in addition to limiting courses of estrogen to 6 to
12 months followed by gradual withdrawal, dosage might be limited
to 3 times weekly on a trial basis. Estrogen should be discontinued

---

* The lowest effective dose is determined by keeping a daily "flush
count" to ascertain the lowest daily dose that will reduce the frequency
and severity of flushes to an acceptable level.

altogether as soon as possible. If only flushes persist beyond 60 years of age, all estrogen should be discontinued. Nonhormonal drugs such as clonidine, ergot preparations and certain sedatives may be substituted for the relief of hot flushes.

3. Although we do not yet have accurate and reliable predictive indicators, an attempt should be made to identify the woman who may be at high risk for the development of osteoporosis. The following features suggest the possibility of increased risk:
   (1) slender build, light-boned, white or Oriental race
   (2) a sedentary life-style or restricted physical activity
   (3) a family history (mother or sister) of osteoporosis (reported by some investigators)
   (4) a low-sodium diet (also likely to be a low-calcium diet)
   (5) heavy smoking
   (6) excessive use of antacids that contain aluminum
   (7) long-term use of cortisone-related drugs
   (8) habitual use of carbonated beverages (reported by some investigators)
   (9) excessive consumption of alcohol
   (10) increased urinary excretion of calcium*

For the woman thought to be at increased risk for the development of osteoporosis, estrogen treatment should be started within 3 years after menstruation ceases. The following schedule of estrogen therapy may be recommended for prevention: conjugated equine estrogens—0.625 mg daily or 3 times weekly, for the first 3 weeks of each month. Periodic examinations as outlined in Part I above should be performed. Estrogen replacement therapy may continue indefinitely, always with appropriate supervision.

In addition to the prudent use of estrogen, regular exercise and a daily intake of 1500 mg of calcium † and 400 units of vitamin D ‡ are generally thought to be beneficial in slowing the development of osteoporosis.

(continued)

* Lactose intolerance and premature menopause (before age 45–50) are also recognized as additional risk factors. —AUTHORS

† About five glasses of milk (preferably skim) or its equivalent in calcium. —AUTHORS

‡ The dose generally found in a multiple-vitamin tablet. —AUTHORS

Conjugated estrogens

The following conjugated estrogens are available for use in treating the menopausal syndrome. These are often called the "natural" estrogens, but they may be derived from natural or synthetic sources.

Conjugated estrogens (Genisis, Premarin)

Esterified estrogens (Evex, Menest)

Estradiol cypionate (Depo-Estradiol, injection)

Estradiol valerate (Delestrogen, injection)

Estriol (Hormonin, a mixture of estriol, estradiol, and estrone)

Piperazine estrone sulfate (Ogen)

Micronized 17-B estradiol (Estrace)

Transdermal estradiol skin patch (Estraderm-50 and 100)

Adapted from The Essential Guide to Prescription Drugs, *fourth edition, and* The Essential Guide to Prescription Drugs 1988 *by James W. Long, M.D. (Harper & Row, 1985, 1988).*

phy or the prevention of osteoporosis, the addition of progestin during a portion of the ERT cycle may help prevent endometrial cancer. However, the long-term effects of progestin in older women are unknown.

Because of the established increased risk of developing endometrial cancer and gallbladder disease as well as the possible risk of developing hypertension, liver problems, and altered blood clotting, all women receiving ERT must have twice-yearly examinations for blood pressure elevation, breast masses, and the development of endometrial hyperplasia as well as endometrial cancer. An endometrial biopsy is recommended before ERT is begun and on a yearly basis thereafter, especially if a woman is receiving estrogen alone. A regular Pap smear should include material from the endocervical canal, since this enhances the otherwise unreliable detection of endometrial cancer. Regular blood tests for glucose, cholesterol, high-density lipoprotein and triglyceride levels, and liver function are also recommended.

Home Remedies. If women are experiencing minimal discomfort and do not wish or are unable to use estrogen, a simple lubricant that dissolves in water (for example, K-Y jelly) can be placed in the vagina before intercourse to reduce dryness and friction. Do *not* use oil-based lubricants such as petroleum jelly, because they do not dissolve in water and can be a vehicle for vaginal infection.

Bacterial or viral cystitis is often preventable or reversible. If there is a predisposition to infection, careful washing of the vaginal area and the penis with soap and water before sexual activity helps reduce the possibility. Older women should urinate before lovemaking since a full bladder is more easily irritated. Immediately after intercourse it is helpful to drink large amounts of water and urinate frequently to flush out any disease agents. If symptoms persist, medical care is necessary.

If home douching is recommended by a physician for a vaginal infection, an ordinary cleansing douche is two tablespoons of white vinegar mixed with two quarts of quite warm—not hot—water. Fill a clean douche bag (or a hot-water bottle with a douching attachment) with the fluid, hang the container a foot or so above the floor of the bathtub and lie down in the tub. Insert the nozzle about an inch and a half into the vagina and *slowly* release the clamp so the water runs in gently and drains back out. Baking soda (one tablespoon per quart of water) is sometimes recommended instead of vinegar; follow the doctor's recommendation. Commercially prepared douches are unnecessary and expensive. A number of them contain substances that can cause irritation or allergic reactions.

The wearing of cotton panties rather than nonabsorbent nylon or other synthetics can help prevent infections by allowing air to circulate in the vaginal area. For the same reason, snug girdles, pantyhose, and tight slacks should not be worn by women susceptible to infection.

Since the clitoral area of older women is often more sensitive to trauma or irritation, sexual partners should be careful to touch this area in a way that does not produce pain. Older women should be frank in telling their partners what is pleasurable and

Preventing Urinary Tract Infections, Treating Mild Infections, and Avoiding Reinfections

1. Drink lots of fluid every day. Try to drink a glass of water every 2 or 3 hours. (For active infection, drink enough to pour out a good stream of urine every hour. It really helps!)

2. Urinate frequently and try to empty your bladder completely each time. Never try to hold your urine once your bladder feels full.

3. Keep the bacteria in your bowels and anus away from your urethra by wiping yourself from front to back after urinating or having a bowel movement. Wash your genitals from front to back with plain water or very mild soap at least once a day.

4. Any sexual activity that irritates the urethra, puts pressure on the bladder, or spreads bacteria from the anus to the vagina or urethra can contribute to cystitis. Make sure that you and your lover have clean hands and genitals before sex, and wash after contact with the anal area before touching the vagina or urethra. To prevent irritation to the urethra, try to avoid prolonged direct clitoral stimulation and pressure on the urethral area during oral-genital sex or masturbation. Make sure your vagina is well lubricated before intercourse. Rear-entry positions and prolonged vigorous intercourse tend to put additional stress on the urethra and bladder. Emptying your bladder before and immediately after sex is a good idea. If you tend to get cystitis after sex despite these precautions, you may want to ask your practitioner for preventive tablets (i.e., sulfa, ampicillin, nitrofurantoin); a single dose of a tablet after sex has been shown effective in preventing infections and is usually not associated with the same negative effects as a prolonged course of antibiotics.

5. Tight jeans, bicycling, or horseback riding may cause trauma to the urethra. When you engage in sports that can provoke cystitis in you, wear loose clothing and try to drink extra water.

6. Caffeine and alcohol irritate the bladder. If you don't want to stop using them, try to drink less of them and drink enough water to dilute them.

7. Some women find that routine use of cranberry juice (preferably the kind without sugar) or vitamin C to make their urine more acid helps to prevent urinary tract problems. (If you have an infection, try combining 500 mg of vitamin C and cranberry juice 4 times a day; you can substitute fresh cranberries in plain yogurt for the juice.) Whole grains, meats, nuts, and many fruits also

help to acidify the urine. Avoid strong spices (curry, cayenne, chili, black pepper).

8. Diets high in refined sugars and starches (white flour, white rice, pasta, etc.) may predispose some women to urinary tract infections.

9. Keep up your resistance by eating and resting well and finding ways to reduce stress in your life as much as possible.

10. Vitamin B$_6$ and magnesium-calcium supplements help to relieve spasm of the urethra, which can predispose you to cystitis. This is especially helpful for women who need to have their urethras dilated repeatedly.

11. If you have an infection, soak in a hot tub 2 or 3 times a day; try a hot-water bottle or heating pad on your abdomen and back.

Adapted from The New Our Bodies, Ourselves *by the Boston Women's Health Book Collective (Simon & Schuster, 1984).*

what is not. The discomfort of "honeymoon cystitis" may be alleviated by changes in sexual positioning. The male partner should thrust his penis downward toward the back of the vagina and in the direction of the rectum, rather than toward the upper part of the vagina. This protects the bladder and delicate urethra.

Older Men

Most men begin to worry secretly about sexual aging some time in their thirties, when they compare their present level of sexual activity with their previous performance as teenagers and very young adults. These worries tend to accelerate in the forties and fifties and reach a peak in the sixties as definite sexual changes continue to be observed.

What changes do men notice? Quite simply, their sexual organs don't work in the same way as they did at a younger age. Lacking understanding of this change, men misinterpret it as alarming evidence of either the onset of impotence or its future inevitability. "From a psychosexual point of view," say Masters and Johnson, "the male over age fifty has to contend with one of the great fallacies of our culture. Every man in this age group is arbitrarily identified by both public and professional alike as sexually impaired."

Potency is the man's sexual capacity for intercourse. Impotence is the temporary or permanent incapacity to have an erection sufficient to carry out the sexual act. (Sterility should not be confused with impotence. It refers to infertility or the incapacity to father children.) What is normal potency for one man may not be normal for another. There are variations in the frequency of erection and the length of time an erection is maintained. Such individual differences often continue over many years, defining unique personal patterns. Therefore comparisons of a man's present sexual status must be made in terms of his past history and not in terms of some generalized "standard" involving comparisons with other men. Most sex therapists do not consider impotence or erectile dysfunction to be a problem unless it occurs in 25 percent or more of sexual encounters with the same partner.

Allowing for individual variation from man to man, a number of gradual and fairly predictable processes are associated with chronological aging. An older man ordinarily takes longer to obtain an erection than a younger man. The difference is a matter of minutes after sexual stimulation rather than a few seconds. The erection may also not be quite as large, straight, and hard as in previous years. Once the man is fully excited, however, his erection will usually be sturdy and reliable, particularly if this was the pattern in earlier life. Increased manual stimulation of the penis is often helpful in promoting and maintaining arousal.

The lubrication that appears prior to ejaculation (Cowper's gland secretory activity) decreases or disappears completely as men age, but this has little effect on sexual performance. There is also a reduction in the volume of seminal fluid, and this results in a decrease in the need to ejaculate. Younger men produce three to five ml of semen (about one teaspoon) every twenty-four hours, while men past fifty produce two to three ml. This can be a decided advantage in lovemaking, since it means that the older man can delay ejaculation more easily and thus make love longer, extending his own enjoyment and enhancing the possibility of orgasm for his partner.

Orgasms may begin to feel different with age. The younger man is aware of a few pleasurable seconds, just before ejaculation, when he can no longer control himself. As ejaculation occurs, powerful contractions are felt and the semen spurts with a force that can carry it one to two feet from the tip of the penis. With an older man there may be a briefer period of awareness before ejaculation or no such period at all. (In some men, however, this period actually lengthens because of spasm in the prostate.) The orgasm itself is generally less explosive, in that semen is propelled a shorter distance and contractions are less forceful. *None* of these physiological changes interfere with the aging man's experiencing extreme orgasmic pleasure, even when the pre-ejaculation stage is altered or completely missing.

The forcefulness of orgasm also lessens naturally when a couple voluntarily prolong their lovemaking before orgasm. Older men have a choice of an extended period of sexual pleasure with a milder orgasm or a briefer session with a more intense orgasm.

Whereas younger men can usually have another ejaculation in a matter of minutes after orgasm, the older man must wait a longer period of time (the refractory period), from several hours up to several days, before an ejaculation is again possible. In addition, the older man may rapidly lose his erection following orgasm, sometimes so quickly that the penis literally slips out of the vagina. This is not a sign of impairment of the penis and its erectile capacity.

Older men need not fall into the common trap of measuring manhood by the frequency with which they can carry intercourse through to ejaculation. Some men over sixty are physically satisfied with one or two ejaculations per week because of the decrease of semen production. Others, particularly if they were sexually less active earlier in life, do not ejaculate this frequently. Whatever the customary frequency, and although they can often force themselves to ejaculate more often, if left to choice each man finds his own level. Remember that lovemaking need not be limited to ejaculatory ability. Men who are knowledgeable and comfortable about themselves may have intercourse as frequently as they wish but ejaculate perhaps only once out of every two or three times that they make love. By delaying ejaculation, the older man may be able to become erect over and over again, continuing with intercourse and the pleasurable feelings it arouses.

Male fertility—sperm production—generally ends in the mid-seventies, though there have been instances where it continued into the nineties. A urologist can test for the presence of live sperm through microscopic examination of semen. It is important enough to bear repeating that fertility has no connection with potency (erectile capacity); even if a man loses his capacity to father children, his ability to have intercourse is not affected by loss of sperm production.

In general, men do not lose their capacity to have erections and ejaculations as they age. The patterns of sexual activity of healthy men as they grow older tend to reflect the patterns earlier in their lives, with the added factor of a somewhat slower physical response due to aging. Problems that may occur, particularly impotence, are caused by physical or psychological difficulties and are frequently treatable. Interest in sex or sexual desire is believed to decline only slightly with age in healthy men, according to current studies. In fact, desire does not necessarily change even in those men who experience a loss of erectile capacity or a change in orgasmic frequency. But the amount of sexual activity itself, beyond normal ejaculatory declines, does tend to decrease. Some speculate that this may be influenced by changes in the central nervous system that reduce the male's ability to translate visual sexual stimuli into physical arousal. Other factors may be disease processes under way but not yet obvious. Finally, the unavailability of one's mate obviously influences sexual activity.

Is There a Male Menopause?

Do men experience a period in life that is physically or psychologically comparable to the female cessation of menstruation and loss of estrogen hormones? There is certainly no physical "menopause" or climacteric in men analogous to that in women, because hormone loss in men does not occur precipitously. (Actually, hormone loss in women occurs in spurts, and never in a single, abrupt cessation.) Decreases in the male hormone testosterone take place very gradually, if at all, with age, and there are wide variations from man to man. Some older men actually have testosterone levels identical with those in young men. Few men have specific physiological symptoms that can be traced directly to lowered testosterone levels. Distinct psychological symptoms are also rare and can usually be accounted for by other circumstances in a man's life, such as his reactions to retirement, to aging in general, or to other stresses.

As research on male hormone levels becomes more sophisticated and reliable, it may eventually be possible to define a male climacteric, particularly with reference to some of the sexual changes that accompany male aging. However, it will be quite different from our concept of female menopause, with far less distinct and less predictable symptoms.

Physical Sexual Changes—Are They Aging or Disease?

We do not yet know whether all the physiological changes we have described in this chapter are "normal aging" processes or symptoms of reversible physical conditions. The fact that a man takes longer to achieve an erection as he gets older, or requires a longer period of time before an erection can occur again after the last sexual act, may possibly be related to reduced nutritive, oxygen and blood supplies because of hardening of the arteries (arteriosclerosis). From a variety of studies we know that much physical change attributed to aging is, in fact, due to a variety of other factors, notably the vascular diseases. The integrative systems of the body that link so many of its functions—the circulatory system, the endocrine (or hormonal) system, the central nervous system—all play a role in the decline of functioning when they are affected by diseases. We are only beginning to have some knowledge of the fundamentals of the aging process itself: whether there is a central-nervous-system pacemaker that dictates change; whether there are reductions in the speed of reactions and in metabolism.

It is possible that in the future we will find sexual activity among older people actually improving as we increasingly separate out the diseases and psychological impairments of old age from the aging processes, and begin to prevent and treat these diseases and impairments on a wide scale. Furthermore, if aging factors become more clear-cut and if agents directly retarding the process of aging are found, there will be still further changes in the sexual picture. What relatively healthy men and women need to remember, even under the limitations of our present knowledge about aging, is that sexual activity—to whatever degree and in whatever forms they want to express it—should continue to be possible, normal, pleasurable, and beneficial. Those older people with fairly common chronic ailments can also adapt their sexual desires to satisfactory expression in many cases. Neither age nor most infirmity automatically spells the end of sex.

Chapter 3

Common Medical Problems and Sex

Illness and Sex

What happens to sexuality when illness strikes? An acute illness that is sudden and severe has an immediate effect. The body becomes totally involved in meeting the physical threat, and anxiety is strong until the crisis has passed and the full extent of the illness is known. Understandably, people in these circumstances have little or no energy and attention left for sexual feelings. Once the acute phase is over, most people return slowly to sexuality; but if recovery time is lengthy or if the illness results in a chronic condition, which must be lived with, there can be problems. We will discuss several of the more common conditions that may directly affect sexuality in people over sixty.

Heart Disease

In the forty-five to sixty-four-year age group the occurrence of heart disease is nearly three times as great in men as in women. After sixty-five the rates become more equal; it is believed the postmenopausal woman is less protected because of the reduction in estrogen levels.

Heart (coronary) attacks lead many people to give up sex altogether under the assumption that it will endanger their lives. Recent studies show that 60 to 75 percent of couples decrease or stop sexual activity after a heart attack, many because their doctors haven't given them adequate advice about sex. Studies also show that the person who does resume sexual activity usually waits about sixteen weeks. Those with the most active sex lives before a coronary resume sex soonest. Many experts believe that an eight- to fourteen-week waiting period is adequate before resumption of sexual intercourse, depending on the patient's interest, general fitness, and conditioning. Self-stimulation or mutual masturbation may be an alternative and usually can be started earlier than sexual intercourse. Some propose a functional test to determine when it is safe to resume: if you can walk briskly for three blocks without distress in the chest, pain, palpitations, or shortness of breath, you are usually well enough for sexual exertion.

Sex can be carried out safely without sacrificing pleasure and quality. Studies tell us that, on the average, couples take ten to sixteen minutes for the sex act. The oxygen usage (or "cost") in sex approximates climbing one or two flights of stairs, walking rapidly at a rate of two to two and a half miles an hour, or completing many common occupational tasks. In average sexual activity the heart rate ranges from 90 to 160 beats a minute, which is the level for light to moderate physical activity. Systolic blood pressure (the upper reading, which reflects the contraction phase of the heart's action) may double, from 120 to over 240, and the respiratory rate rises from sixteen or eighteen to about sixty breaths a minute. These vital signs increase only slightly more in men than in women, perhaps due in part to the usual sexual position of the man on top. Intercourse conducted side by side or with the woman on top can help to reduce the exertion of the man if he is the one with the heart problem. These positions avoid sapping of energy from prolonged use of the arms and legs to support the body. Proper physical conditioning (usually a program of brisk walking and/or swimming) under the doctor's guidance can also be useful, in part because the pulse-rate rise during sex can be lowered by conditioning.

Physical-fitness programs enhance heart performance for a variety of activities, including sex. Isometric exercises may be unwise for certain kinds of patients because they cause pressure changes in the aorta, the major blood vessel from the heart. Check with your physician. Before undertaking an exercise program you can ask your doctor to arrange special testing in which an electrocardiogram, or EKG (a tracing of the heart's electric currents that provides information regarding the heart's actions in health and disease) is taken while you are conducted through various levels of exercise. An electromagnetic tape recording of your EKG during the sexual act can even be made in your own home. This is called Hellerstein's Sexercise Tolerance Test. Drs. H. E. Hellerstein and E. H. Friedman studied the sexual activity of men after recovery from an acute heart attack by monitoring sexual activities in the privacy of their patients' homes. They reported that if the patient could perform exercise at levels of vigorous walking and other special activities without symptoms of abnormal pulse rate, blood pressure, or EKG changes, it was generally safe to recommend the resumption of sexual activity.

Some physicians warn that such stress tests are not infallible. They can produce false alarms for healthy people, while coronary disease may not be registered. A medical and sexual history, the patient's report on chest pain during exertion, as well as an electrocardiogram taken during rest should all be part of the stress examination.

It must be remembered that physical exercise leads to less likelihood of a heart attack. The sedentary person may be more prone to coronary attacks and less apt to survive the experience if one occurs. Too much food and drink before sexual intercourse can also place a strain on the heart. Of course, if the condition of the heart has deteriorated to the point that an attack is imminent, it will occur with any physical exertion, not merely sex. Many everyday nonsexual activities that people are not likely to give up produce a greater increase in heart and respiratory rates than sexual intercourse.

It should also be realized that sexual arousal alone (without intercourse) affects the vital signs—although not as intensely as

the sexual act itself. Failure to provide sexual release may prolong arousal, causing psychological frustration that will probably
produce some adverse physical effects.

Potency problems can follow a heart attack for both physical
and psychological reasons. A man may experience chest pain
(angina pectoris) during various forms of exertion, including sex,
that frightens him and prevents erection. To counteract this pain,
coronary dilators such as nitroglycerin, prescribed by a physician, can be taken to improve circulation and reduce pain just
prior to intercourse. A second common and understandable
cause of impotence is fear of inducing another coronary and risk-
ing death. Yet the incidence of death during intercourse is estimated at less that 1 percent of sudden coronary deaths. (In one
major study the rate was less than 0.3 percent!) Of this small
percentage, seven out of ten deaths occur in extramarital relations, suggesting that the stressful aspects associated with such
affairs, such as hurry, guilt, and anxiety, may play a role.

Depression and anxiety are common after a heart attack.
Irritability, exhaustion, and feelings of loss may be present. Patients may believe that their partners are no longer attracted to
them. Conversely, partners may become overly protective and
fearful of upsetting patients. In most cases, all these normal
reactions to what has been a frightening experience will subside
with time. Talking about such feelings with the physician or with
a psychotherapist can offer relief and may help to avoid problems
with the relationship and with sex.

Physicians, however, do not always advise their patients adequately on the resumption of sexual activity after a heart attack.
They may be too conservative or fail to realize the importance of
sex to the patient. If you want to know more than your doctor
has told you, it may be necessary to ask for specific information
and directions, including a program of physical conditioning. Your
sex partner also needs to be fully informed and counseled about
any changes in life-style, including lovemaking, that may be necessary. *Under most circumstances there is little reason to abstain
from sex after a heart attack and many reasons to continue.* Plea-

sure, exhilaration, release of tension, mild exercise, and a sense of well-being are some of the benefits. However, after the resumption of sexual activity, the patient should report the following to his or her doctor: (1) anginal pain occurring during or after sex; (2) palpitations continuing fifteen minutes or more afterward; (3) unusual episodes of sleeplessness after sexual exertion; (4) marked fatigue the next day. Stress can be lessened by: (1) having a familiar and considerate partner; (2) waiting three hours or more after eating or drinking alcohol; (3) using a room with a moderate temperature; (4) choosing a relaxed time, such as the morning after a restful night. If the patient begins to feel strained or anxious during sexual activity, he or she should simply stop and breathe deeply for a few minutes before beginning again.

Episodes of congestive heart failure are also commonly called heart attacks. When they are compensated for by digitalis, diuretics, and diet, sex is again an active possibility. Two to three weeks for recovery are advised before resuming sex.

Patients with cardiac pacemakers need not give up sex unless the condition of the heart itself precludes such activity. Limitations on all forms of physical activity are advised during the first two weeks following implantation to allow healing. Otherwise the guidelines to follow will vary based on evaluation of the underlying cardiac condition.

Coronary Bypass Surgery. Because of symptoms, treatment of the disease, or fear of sudden death from sexual activity, many patients have sexual dysfunction by the time they have coronary bypass surgery. After surgery, patients must learn what level of activity they can undertake without danger of stressing the chest bones. Most patients are advised to walk and move about very soon after the surgery. Exercise programs that improve heart capacity can be reassuring to patients who fear resuming sexual activity.

Psychological dependence on nitroglycerin before sexual activity is common, even though surgery may have eliminated the need for it. Support may be obtained from other patients who have successfully weaned themselves from nitrogylcerin, or, failing this, a mild antianxiety medication used for a brief time may be helpful.

Those who require medications such as beta blockers, which can decrease sexual desire and cause impotence, may be able to switch to other medications, such as calcium blockers like verapamil, with fewer sexual side effects. Those with arrhythmias (irregular heartbeat) that do not require treatment need reassurance and perhaps a heart monitor (the Holter monitor) or a treadmill test to calm anxiety about sexual activity. When antiarrhythmic drugs and beta blockers cannot be avoided, patients need to understand that such drugs are life-protective, and when they interfere with sexual desire and performance, other forms of intimacy and physical pleasure are possible.

Most coronary bypass surgery patients can expect to return to a reasonable level of sexual activity. An exercise and conditioning program can improve their chances. *Short-term* treatment of anxiety and depression with appropriate drugs can be helpful in leading toward resumption of sexual functioning, but in the long run counseling, psychotherapy, and information about heart attacks are more effective treatment methods.

Hypertension

It is safe for most patients with hypertension—high blood pressure—to have sex. (Many people with hypertension have no significant impairment of heart function.) As a general rule, patients with average to moderate hypertension, men or women, need not restrict themselves sexually. They should, however, have their hypertension well controlled by diet, physical exercise, and, when appropriate, drug therapy. Very severe cases of hypertension may require some modification of sexual activity; your doctor is the best judge of this.

Men with untreated hypertension are reported to have about a 15 percent incidence of impotence. Sexual impairment can be avoided by proper treatment of hypertension: weight loss if one is overweight, regular exercise, reduction of cholesterol levels, limitation of salt to five grams or less a day, moderate use of alcohol, and no smoking are the first steps in treatment. If these do not bring blood pressure down to acceptable levels, medication is necessary. Such medication must be carefully chosen to avoid side effects of impaired sexual response (see page 64).

Stroke

Unless a stroke (cerebrovascular accident) causes severe trauma to the brain, sexual desire often remains undamaged; performance is more likely to be affected. However, strokes do not necessitate the discontinuance of sexual activity. If paralysis has occurred, appropriate sexual positions can be chosen to compensate for it. A useful reference for stroke patients and their partners is D. C. Renshaw's article "Sexual Problems in Stroke Patients" in the journal *Medical Aspects of Human Sexuality,* December 1975 (available in medical libraries). It is important to know that sexual activity has not been found to be a factor in bringing on a stroke or in causing more damage to those who have had a stroke.

Diabetes

Sugar diabetes (diabetes mellitus) is common in late life. Most men with diabetes are *not* impotent, but it is one of the few illnesses that can directly cause chronic impotence in men. Impotence occurs two to five times as often in diabetics as in the general population, even though sexual interest and desire may continue. Indeed, impotence is often the first symptom of diabetes.

Most cases of diabetes-produced impotence are reversible. If the disease has been poorly controlled, there is a fair chance that proper regulation thereafter will improve potency. When impotence occurs in well-controlled diabetes, it may be permanent.

(Unfortunately, if you have been diabetic for a long time, the chances are greater that the impotence will be chronic and irreversible.)

It is more difficult to evaluate the effects of diabetes on the sexuality of women since they do not have an obvious physical indicator like erection. However, current research strongly suggests that sexuality is affected far less by diabetes in women than in men.

Chronic Prostatitis

Diminished sexual desire in men may be associated with chronic prostatitis. This disease is an inflammation of the prostate gland, a walnut-sized organ located just beneath the bladder in the male. It produces the milky lubricating fluid that transports sperm during sexual intercourse. Prostatitis is characterized by a history of cloudy white discharge from the penis, usually in the morning or while straining on the toilet. Pain may be present in the perineal region (the area between the scrotum and the anus) and in the end of the penis on urination and ejaculation. Manual manipulation of the prostate causes tenderness. Treatment includes antibiotics, warm sitz baths, and periodic gentle prostatic massage by a physician. Sexual desire usually returns after pain lessens, especially when the pain after ejaculation is eliminated.

Many doctors believe prostatitis can be caused by both too frequent and too infrequent sex. The basis for some pain between the anus and the scrotum after ejaculation may be mild prostatitis; other causes are congestion due to excessive or lengthy preliminary sexual arousal, or an unsatisfying orgasm. However, a more common cause is infrequent sex, which results in congestion in the pelvic area. Treatment in these cases consists of more frequent ejaculation as well as prostatic massage and warm sitz baths. Some believe that the practice of Kegel exercises (see pages 85–86) may help.

Whenever chronic prostatitis is a possibility, one should avoid excessive alcohol. Should urinary retention develop following sexual intercourse, as it occasionally does, it may be caused by the combination of a large fluid intake and the sedative effect of alcohol. If there is also some enlargement of the prostate without inflammation, excessive fluid intake, including alcohol, may lead to retention of urine.

It has recently been discovered that up to half or more of prostate infections are caused by the major U.S. venereal disease chlamydia and are transmitted by sexual contact. Once diagnosed, this bacterium responds to antibiotics.

Arthritis

Arthritis is a widespread condition that affects forty million Americans and strikes women twice as often as men. Rheumatoid arthritis, commonly beginning between ages twenty-five and fifty, and osteoarthritis, a later-life condition, are the two major forms of arthritis and may cause pain during sexual activity. Medications such as simple aspirin are used to reduce pain. It is reassuring to know that most drugs used to treat arthritis, except for corticosteroids, do not interfere with either sexual desire or sexual performance. Experimentation with new sexual positions that do not aggravate pain in sensitive joints is often helpful. A well-established program of exercise, rest, and warm baths is especially useful in reducing arthritic discomfort and in facilitating sex. Indeed, much of the crippling by rheumatoid arthritis results from inactivity. A person tends to keep painful joints in comfortable positions, and they become stiffened, even "frozen." For information on exercise and other treatments, write for the free publication list published by the Arthritis Foundation, 115 East 18th Street, New York, NY 10003. Several reprints on sexuality and arthritis are also available.

Hip discomfort is perhaps the most frequent arthritic problem that affects sexual activity. Hip action during sex may be slowed down or made difficult because of pain or changes in the ability to move the hips. When the problem is severe, surgical hip replacement may restore function, including that involved in sex. For less severe conditions, a range of therapies can be beneficial. Exercise, prescribed by your doctor, should include a full range of motion for the joints, strengthening and stretching of muscles, and engaging in the usual household and outside activities. It is also important to maintain an erect position when standing and walking, sit upright in a straightback chair, and rest in bed for short periods several times during the day. In general, those with this problem should rest or sleep in a straight position, flat on the back, using a small pillow under the head (a pillow under the knees can lead to stiff, bent knees).

Heat relaxes muscle spasm and is useful before undertaking an exercise program and also prior to sex. Various types of heat can be used, such as heat lamps, heating pads, warm compresses, tub baths, showers, and paraffin baths. A daily tub bath with warm—but not hot—water and for no more than twenty minutes is excellent. (Longer than that can be fatiguing.) The use of a water bed and massage oils may enhance comfort. During sexual activity the side-by-side position—either face to face or back to front—may be preferred by both men and women, especially when the patient has many tender areas and pain trigger points. Experiment until you find positions that work best for you. Pillows can help cushion painful joints.

Timing can also be important. Some discover that pain and stiffness diminish or disappear completely at certain times of day; sexual activity can be planned for these times. Those with rheumatoid arthritis often feel greater pain and stiffness in the morning, while for those with osteoarthritis, morning is usually the best time of day, with discomfort increasing at the end of the day. Ask your doctor to time pain or anti-inflammatory medications so they will be most effective at times when you are most likely to have sexual activity. A condition known as Sjögren's syndrome occurs with some forms of arthritis and results in a decrease in body secretions. A lubricant like K-Y jelly will compensate for inadequate vaginal secretions.

There is evidence that regular sexual activity may produce some relief from the pain of rheumatoid arthritis for four to eight hours, probably because of adrenal gland production of the hormone cortisone and because of the physical activity involved. The body's release of endorphins, its natural pain relievers, during sexual activity and especially during orgasm may also be a factor. Finally, emotional stress can result from sexual dissatisfaction, and since stress worsens arthritis, satisfying sexual activity can be helpful in maintaining good functioning.

Backache

Backache in the small of the back near the base of the spine is common among older people. Perhaps the most frequent cause is strain produced by sudden use of back muscles in a generally inactive person. In women it can be caused by osteoporosis (postmenopausal softening of the bones), related to reduction of estrogen levels. Slipped discs and arthritis are other causes of backache in both men and women.

A firm mattress and bed board are needed by most backache sufferers. A plywood board at least one-half inch thick and the same size as the mattress can be placed between the mattress and springs for extra support. Exercise is helpful for most forms of backache, but you should see your doctor for instructions in your particular case. Slipped discs often respond well to exercise but sometimes may require prolonged bed rest; otherwise surgery may be necessary. Sufferers from arthritic backache should follow the program described above for arthritis. Sexual activity itself is an excellent form of exercise therapy for the back, stomach, and pelvic muscles, and if undertaken in a regular and reasonably vigorous manner can help reduce back pain. During sex, the side position may be most comfortable if back muscles are tender. Or the backache sufferer may prefer lying on his or her back, with the partner on top. Areas of discomfort can be supported by pillows.

Anemia

One out of four people over sixty has some measure of anemia, a common cause of fatigue and consequent reduction of sexual activity. Anemia may develop insidiously following even a mild general or localized infection, or as a result of a poor diet.

Tiredness, loss of appetite, and headaches are some of its early symptoms. Since anemia is the symptom of a number of diseases, comprehensive medical examination is indicated. Follow-up treatment is important. Often an improved diet with adequate vitamins and minerals is all that is necessary to restore both energy and sexual activity.

Chronic Cystitis and Urethritis

Some women experience recurrent outbreaks of cystitis and urethritis following intercourse. The cause is often unclear. The chief symptoms are severe pain and burning around the urethra. If no organisms can be found in their urine, such women are often told their problem is psychological. This leads to outrage at the doctor and to depression, continued pain, and a sense of hopelessness.

Do not give up. The diagnostic process may have to be ongoing until the cause or causes are found and corrected. The merits of surgical correction, medications, education on sexual techniques and positions, pain management, and interpersonal counseling should all be weighed. A woman's sexual partner should be checked for possible untreated prostatitis. The depression that usually accompanies chronic cystitis needs to be dealt with. Above all, the physician should persist, and the woman should not be told it is all in her head. Even long-standing cystitis can be evaluated and cured.

Stress Incontinence

Some women develop stress incontinence (caused by stretched pelvic muscles), a condition in which there is a seepage of urine because of a momentary inability to control the bladder. This happens particularly when they laugh, cough, engage in sex, or otherwise exert themselves. Dyspareunia, or painful intercourse, may also be present. Stress incontinence is most frequently seen in women who have had a number of children, sometimes with unrepaired injuries following childbirth, with resulting relaxation of the supports of the uterus and bladder. It is also seen in women who have had the uterus removed surgically (hysterectomy). Slack supporting tissues may cause the bladder to protrude into the vagina (cystocele). Inserting a large tampon in the vagina, which gives support to the bladder, can sometimes provide temporary relief of this form of mild incontinence. To guard against toxic shock syndrome, the tampon should not be left in place for more than a few hours. Estrogen taken by mouth or applied locally in the form of cream may help firm up the vaginal lining and thus reduce the irritation from the protruding bladder. Special exercises, called Kegel exercises (described on pages 85–86), are very useful.

Biofeedback training may bring improvement. In severe cases, surgery may be required to reposition the internal pelvic organs and tighten muscles. Such surgery can be done under local or spinal anesthesia, and the surgical success rate is very high. A self-help and advocacy organization called HIP (Help for Incontinent People) can provide information and lists of resources. Write to HIP, P.O. Box 544, Union, SC 29379, and include a business-size, self-addressed, stamped envelope.

Herniation, or prolapse of the uterus and of the rectum (rectocele), may occur alone or in association with prolapse of the bladder. Surgical treatment is usually effective.

Parkinson's Disease

Parkinson's disease is a progressive nervous-system disorder of the later years marked by tremor, slowness of movement, partial facial paralysis, and peculiarity of posture and gait. Depression is commonly associated with Parkinson's disease and may lead to impotence in men and lack of sexual interest in both sexes. When there is advanced organic involvement, however, impotence may be physically connected with the disease. Patients with Parkinson's disease who are treated with drugs such as L-dopa may show improved sexual performance, largely because of their generally increased sense of well-being and greater mobility.

Peyronie's Disease

This disorder, found in men, produces an upward bowing of the penis with the shaft angled to the right or left. A fibrous thickening of the walls of the blood vessels (corpora cavernosa) of the penis produces the symptoms, but its cause is unknown. Results of treatment are not predictable. Symptoms sometimes disappear spontaneously after four years or so. One therapy is p-aminobenzoate (in the form of Potaba or Potaba Plus) for about six months. Application of ultrasound to the fibrous areas of the penis in order to disrupt fibrous tissue has been successful with some patients, particularly those who have not had the problem for long. Surgical removal of the plaque is often successful. Cortisone is sometimes effective, but it must be injected rather than taken orally. There is no evidence that vitamin E works.

Intercourse can be painful and, if the penis is angled too far, impossible. However, in most cases of Peyronie's disease sex can continue. This ailment is thought to be rare, but our own experience in talking with physicians and patients leads us to suspect it may be more common than is believed.

Chronic Renal Disease

Patients with chronic renal disease experience a continuum of treatments that may end with renal dialysis or renal transplants. This can be a stressful disease, often associated with depression and anxiety. Male chronic renal patients are often sterile and may have reduced levels of serum testosterone. Other organic factors affecting sexuality may be present, although they have not been identified. Nonetheless, not all renal patients have sexual problems, and those who do may be treatable if the problems are not strictly organic. Treatment of anxiety and depression and the use of marital counseling can be effective. Kidney transplants often restore sexual capacity.

Chronic Emphysema and Bronchitis

Chronic emphysema and bronchitis, which entail shortness of breath, often hinder physical activity, including sex. The extent of the limitation depends on the severity of the disease. Resting at intervals, and finding the least physically taxing ways to have sex, help.

Hernia or Rupture

A hernia or rupture is the protrusion of a part of the intestine through a gap or weak point in the muscular abdominal wall that contains it. The main complication to avoid is strangulation, or cutting off of the blood supply with resulting death of tissue, which is a true surgical emergency. Straining of any kind, including straining during sexual intercourse, can sometimes increase hernia symptoms such as pain and, rarely, induce strangulation. Many surgeons recommend corrective surgery early rather than waiting for an emergency to arise.

If you have had to abstain from sex for a medical reason for any length of time, some readjustment will be necessary when sexual activity is resumed. Irregular or infrequent sexual stimulation can interfere with healthy sexual functioning, adversely affecting potency in men and lubrication, vaginal shape, and muscle tone in women. These difficulties are likely to taper off as activity is resumed, and one should not be discouraged by initial difficulties. When a sexual partner is not available (as, for example, in widowhood) or circumstances do not permit contact with a partner, both men and women can protect much of their sexual capacity through regular self-stimulation (masturbation) if this is acceptable and comfortable for them.

Impotence Based on Physical Causes

What Is Impotence?

We refer here to impotence as erectile dysfunction—that is, the loss of a man's ability to obtain an erection sufficient to achieve or maintain sexual intercourse. (The terms "impotence" and "erection problem" will be used interchangeably.) Rarely do men lose totally the capacity for at least some degree of erection; most have "erection problems," which interfere with full sexual expression. The severity of impotence ranges from incapacity for total erection some of the time to incapacity most or all of the time. Impotence also refers to the inability to sustain an erection even if one is initially able to have one. It is estimated that about ten million American men—one out of eight—suffer from chronic erection problems or impotence. This is *not* part of the normal physical process of growing older, even though problems may increase with age, due to physical illness and other causes. If impotence regularly occurs, one should investigate the cause or causes and treat the condition. Many cases—perhaps the majority—can be improved or even reversed with proper diagnosis and treatment. Therefore it is imperative for a man to be examined medically first to determine whether or not a physical condition is acting as a partial or complete cause of his impotence.

What Produces an Erection?

The physiology and psychology of getting and maintaining an erection are complicated and are based on reflexes rather than consciously controlled by the man himself. Two sets of messages —stimulation of the penis through touch and/or stimulation of the brain through erotic thoughts triggered by sights, smells, hearing, fantasies, or memories—are sent to nerve centers in the spinal cord. These nerve centers send messages to the pelvic blood vessels, causing them to enlarge and fill with blood (engorge), creating an erection. Some believe special valves in the penis close to retain engorgement. Testosterone and chemicals known as neurotransmitters play an important but still unclear role. Mental stimulation alone is often enough to produce erections in adolescents and very young men. But most men in their late forties and thereafter need tactile stimulation of the penis, in addition to erotic thoughts, before erection occurs.

At What Age Are Erection Problems Likely to Occur?

There has been little reliable scientific information concerning the actual experience of impotence as men grow older. Kinsey documented a decline in potency with age up until the age of fifty, but his sample over fifty was too small to draw conclusions from. Duke University and the Gerontology Research Center of the National Institute on Aging in Baltimore have found a general pattern of decline as well, but with much individual variation. Indeed, a significant proportion of men had stable and even rising patterns of sexual activity with age. For our purposes here, it is clear that erection problems do increase with age (due to illness or other causes—but not due to physical aging itself); however, they are not inevitable, nor are they by any means always permanent.

The Mind-Body Issue in Impotence

It has long been generally accepted that at least 90 percent of impotence in men over sixty was psychologically based, with only about 10 percent physiologically caused. These figures, quoted since the 1920s, can be traced back to the book *Impotence in the Male,* by one of Freud's colleagues, William Stekel. William Masters and Virginia Johnson, pioneer sex researchers, arrived at the same conclusions in their laboratory studies of older men, and psychotherapists and sex counselors since have promulgated these beliefs. The proportion of psychologically based impotence among men forty to sixty has been estimated to be even higher, at 95 percent. However, more effective diagnostic techniques and a growing understanding of the physiology of impotence are changing those views. In the last few years, biomedical researchers, using a variety of more sophisticated measurements and advanced techniques, including sleep studies, have begun to suspect that impotence may have a much higher physiological component, perhaps involving 50 percent of all cases of impotence (five million men), regardless of age. The rates may be even higher for older men, especially those with vascular problems.

In this book, we have made an artificial division between physically based and psychologically based impotence, to facilitate discussion. In truth the two are usually intermixed, with a greater emphasis in one direction or another. The psychological aspects of impotence are discussed in other chapters.

Major Causes of Physically Based Impotence

In a significant number of cases of impotence, it is likely that physical illness has been undetected or at least that a mixed diagnosis involving physical as well as emotional components has been overlooked. This helps to explain the estimated 60 percent or higher failure rate from using psychotherapy alone to treat potency problems. The major causes of the approximately five million cases of primarily physically based impotence are listed in the table on the next page.

Diagnostic procedures may require any or all of the following:

▶ A thorough history, including the patient's past sex life, possible psychiatric and psychological contributors to the impotence, review of alcohol and drug use, and past or present illnesses.
▶ A physical examination.
▶ A sleep study, which monitors erections during sleep. Minimal erections or the absence of erections during sleep strongly suggests, but does not definitely prove, an organic basis for impotence. For information on clinics that conduct such studies contact the Association of Sleep Disorders Centers, 604 Second Street, S.W., Rochester, MN 55902.

Physical problem	Cases of impotence (approximate)
Diabetes mellitus	2,000,000 (or more)
Vascular insufficiency (arteriosclerosis, hypertension, antihypertensive medications [beta blocker agents])	1,500,000
Radical surgery (prostatectomies, colostomies, cystectomies, etc.)	650,000
Trauma (spinal cord injuries, pelvic fractures, etc.)	400,000
Hypogonadism and other endocrine disorders	300,000
Multiple sclerosis	180,000
Peyronie's disease (fibrous cavernitis)	Unknown
Side effects from medications (estrogens, anticholinergic drugs, excessive tranquilizers, antidepressants, antihypertensive agents, opiates, alcohol, etc.)	Unknown

▸ Testing of impotence through other methods includes visual stimulation, the use of a vibrator, and a papaverine injection directly into the penis. Papaverine produces an erection lasting three to four hours in patients who are sexually excited *and* physiologically normal. (This can be very effective psychologically, showing a patient with psychological impotence that he can have an erection.) Penile blood measurements may be useful, as well as glucose tolerance tests to rule diabetes in or out.

Treatment for Impotence

Medical treatment for impotence includes treatment of specific underlying diseases and, occasionally, successful treatment with hormones. At present, male hormone therapy (sex-steroid replacement) is controversial and experimental. Replacement of the male hormone testosterone has little known permanent beneficial effect on the sexual problems of older men, particularly impotence, unless there is definitely proven testicular deficiency in the production of male hormones—such as in hypogonadism, a rare condition. Any benefit from testosterone should show up in three to four weeks, but even in those men who do appear to respond to such treatment, improvement is generally short-lived. Beneficial effects do not tend to be maintained indefinitely despite continued hormone administration except in clear-cut deficiencies. There may be side effects such as fluid retention, and evidence indicates that testosterone may stimulate already existing prostatic growth; thus it should not be given if the prostate gland is enlarged.

Currently, no medication can safely be prescribed to correct vascular-disease-related impotence, but studies under way suggest that drugs may be produced that could be injected directly into the penis to improve blood flow.

Nerve damage to the penis as the result of spinal cord injury, lumbar disc disease, radical pelvic surgery, multiple sclerosis, or juvenile-onset diabetes can cause impotence by impeding blood flow. Boston University Medical Center urologist Irwin Goldstein has successfully treated some patients by injecting combined papaverine hydrochloride and phentolamine mesylate into the penis. Prolonged erections were a side effect with some hypertensive individuals.

Although rare, zinc deficiency in the daily diet may interfere with normal hormone production and therefore affect sexual functioning. Zinc can easily be obtained in shellfish, seafood, meats, and certain whole grains, nuts, and legumes, or in multiple vitamins.

Permanent penile prostheses or implants have been surgically inserted in a limited number of American men. These have been used to treat permanent organic impotence, especially due to diabetes, and in a few instances, psychological impotence that has not responded to psychotherapy. The prosthesis serves mainly to enhance a man's self-esteem and possibly improve his partner's pleasure. It does not in itself produce a climax for the man or increase sexual desire. However, those men who could have an orgasm before surgery can do so afterward. The four main manufacturers of prostheses are American Medical Systems, Surgiteck, Mentor, and Dacomed, all of Minneapolis. They will provide information about their products in response to letters and calls. A prosthesis may be implanted in the penis as an inflatable device (such as the Scott inflatable prosthesis) or a silicon rod with a core of either silicon sponge (such as the Small-Carrion semirigid rod prosthesis) or silver wire (such as the Jonas silicon-silver prosthesis).

The following guidelines will help a man and his doctor reach a decision about the desirability of a penile implant. Not considered good candidates for penile prosthesis are men with:

▶ Untreated acute and severe depression. The depression should be successfully treated first.
▶ Serious psychosis or brain disease.
▶ Severe personality disorders, including the chronically dissatisfied.
▶ Severe and complicated marital problems.
▶ Impotence that is not clearly organic.
▶ Health conditions that contraindicate elective surgery.

A penile implant may be advisable when:

▶ It is clear that the impotence is primarily a chronic organic problem (caused, for example, by diabetes, vascular disease, problems associated with rectal or prostate surgery, pelvic nerve injury, or spinal cord injury).
▶ Sexual desire is strong and intercourse is greatly valued by both partners.
▶ There is evidence of continuing sexual activity between the partners even in the absence of sexual intercourse.
▶ The presence of impotence per se is having a destructive effect on the relationship.
▶ The couple have a realistic understanding of what may be achieved, and both approve of the surgery.

Inclusion of partners in pre- and postsurgical evaluation is important. Sex counseling in addition to surgery may be helpful, since couples often need explicit instruction on how best to use a prosthesis.

Risk factors for all implants include the slight danger of infection at the time of insertion and the possibility of mechanical malfunction. In spite of this, estimates of current surgical success in implants are reported to be as high as 90 percent. However, patient and partner satisfaction may be significantly lower than this, particularly over time. Some question any use of permanent prostheses, believing that sexual counseling could help couples find sexual satisfaction with techniques other than vaginal penetration by the penis.

Arteriosclerosis and conditions such as peripheral vascular disease, sickle cell anemia, traumas or accidents to the penis and surrounding area, or simply an insufficient blood flow to the penis since birth can affect blood circulation to the penis. Revascularization, or surgery involving the shifting of blood vessels, is used to restore normal blood circulation to the penis. It is still in the experimental stage, but shows promise. Revascularization is almost never recommended for diabetic impotence. Some surgeons feel revascularization is not indicated in cases of advanced general arteriosclerosis. Others believe that arteriosclerosis often advances segmentally, and if it is more advanced in the penis than in other parts of the body, revascularization in that area may result in many more years of functioning. In one vascular condition, Leriche's syndrome, there is an intermittent reduction of the penile blood supply needed for erection. Aching, fatigue, weakness, cramping, numbness, discomfort in the thigh, pain in the calf, or limping may accompany this syndrome. Many of the symptoms are relieved by rest. Surgery can eliminate the limp and also restore sexual potency.

Vacuum-constriction (V-C) devices for obtaining and maintaining erections are being tested by researchers. A plastic-cylinder vacuum device is fitted over the unerect penis, a piece of plastic tubing is attached to an opening in the end of the device, and a gentle vacuum is produced by sucking out the air with a syringe or with one's mouth. The vacuum encourages blood flow into the penis, creating an erection. Once a full erection occurs, a wide rubber band stored on the end of the cylinder nearest the base of the penis is slipped around the penis to retain the blood there, maintaining the erection. Compared to an implant, this method requires no surgery, is much less expensive, and the penis is not permanently altered. However, the V-C device is relatively new and untested.

Because impotence is such a widespread concern, a host of questionable treatments have evolved. Folklore is full of reputed "remedies." Doctors have been known to prescribe oysters, greens, and massive amounts of vitamins B_{12} and E. There are also "youth doctors" and nonmedical entrepreneurs who produce and sell countless substances and gadgets advertised to rejuvenate sexual potency. Older people are particular targets of fraudulent consumer schemes and devices that promise to "make you look younger" and "guarantee" to prevent or cure impotence. The U.S. Postal Service, which brings action against people engaged in obtaining money or property through the mails by means of false representations, provided us with a representative list of worthless nostrums and alleged aphrodisiacs. Among the popular names are "Mexican Spanish Fly in Liquid Form," "Instant Love Potion," "Sex Stimulant for Women," "Mad Dog Weed," "Magic Lure," "Super Nature Tablets," "European Love Drops," "Linga Pendulum Penis Enlarger and Strengthener," "Big Ox," made of vitamins and minerals, and VBE-21, advertised as the "Doctor's Pill for Loss of Sex Drive." On the next page we list by popular and scientific names a variety of alleged aphrodisiacs. Watch out for them. If they seem to work, it is only through the power of suggestion and any "cure" is likely to be temporary. Some are extremely dangerous; Spanish fly, for example, can kill.

The Food and Drug Administration (FDA) began an attempt to ban the sale of all nonprescription aphrodisiacs in mid-1985. The ban does not, however, cover products like ginseng that do not claim to be aphrodisiacs but nevertheless have that associa-

Some false aphrodisiacs

Alcohol	Especially wines
Cantharidin	Tincture of *Cantharis vesicatoria* (Spanish fly)
Capsicum	Extract of *Capsicum frutescens* (cayenne pepper from South America)
Cimicifugin	Resin from *Cimicifuga racemosa* (black snakeroot)
Cubeb	Oleoresin from *Piper cubeba* (from Java)
Damiana	From leaves of *Turnera diffusa* (from Mexico)
Ergot	Alkaloids from *Claviceps purpurea*
Marijuana	*Cannabis sativa*
Nux vomica	Extract from seeds of *Strychnos nux-vomica*
Sanguinaria	Extract from *Sanguinaria canadenis* (bloodroot)
Vitamin E	d-Alpha-tocopherol

tion in the public mind. Chinese ginseng, readily available in health food stores, is used in the belief that it preserves health, increases alertness, and improves endurance. The aphrodisiac action of ginseng has been interpreted (but not scientifically proven) to be a consequence of improved health, which produces a return to normal sexual desire and functioning. Taken in moderation, ginseng has no known adverse side effects.

One aphrodisiac that may at least partially live up to its reputation and, after studies, eventually graduate to the role of a tested drug is yohimbine, an extract from the bark of the African yohimbe tree. Yohimbine, an alpha blocker, induces dilation of certain blood vessels in the penis. Its also increases release of norepinephrine, a substance that is helpful in producing erections.

Many large medical centers and Veterans Administration hospitals provide information and treatment centers for impotence. Other sources of information or counseling are listed below.

▶ Impotents Anonymous, 119 South Ruth Street, Maryville, TN 37801, has about a hundred chapters. For information, send a stamped, self-addressed envelope.

▶ Recovery of Male Potency is associated with twenty-three U.S. hospitals. Contact Grace Hospital ROMP Center, 18700 Meyers Road, Detroit, MI 48235; (800)835-7667 and (313)966-3219.

▶ Impotence Information Center, Department USA, P.O. Box 9, Minneapolis, MN 55440; (800)843-4315, is run by a maker of penile prostheses.

▶ American Association of Sex Educators, Counselors and Therapists, 11 Dupont Circle, N.W., Suite 220, Washington, DC 20036, publishes a register of its members by state and city.

▶ American Urological Association, 1120 North Charles Street, Baltimore, MD 21201, is a professional organization.

AIDS and Other Sexually Transmitted Diseases

Twenty-five or so diseases are known to spread through sexual contact. Incidence of sexually transmitted diseases has increased steadily in the United States over the past fifteen years, due to the greater number and variety of sexual practices, to a population that moves about readily, and to the emergence of strains of sexually transmitted organisms that are resistant to antibiotics. As a result, we find ourselves in a peculiar position, with growing acceptance of many sexual practices countered by a growing worry about the possibility of acquiring a sexually transmittable disease, especially currently incurable ones like genital herpes and AIDS. People who are single, divorced, separated, or not monogamous in their marriages are beginning to change their sexual behavior because of fear of AIDS. Most of those who have changed are using condoms more frequently, and over 90 percent are more careful about choosing partners and avoiding casual sex or promiscuity.

Acquired Immune Deficiency Syndrome (AIDS)

AIDS, a disease that destroys the body's immune system, is caused by a blood-borne virus known as HTLV-III or HIV (human immunodeficiency virus) and is transmitted by the exchange of certain body fluids, especially through sexual contact that involves an open blood channel in either mucous membranes or broken skin, and through intravenous (IV) drug use. Casual, nonsexual contact is not thought to transmit AIDS. Although low concentrations of the AIDS virus have been found in tears, urine, and saliva, there have been no documented cases of AIDS transmission by these routes. The primary and perhaps sole agents of transmission are HIV-infected blood and semen.

As of this writing over 70 percent of AIDS cases have been homosexual or bisexual men. Intravenous drug users who have shared needles or syringes account for approximately 25 percent of AIDS cases. Hemophiliacs who contracted the disease through blood transfusion or the use of blood products that help blood clot account for a very small percentage of reported AIDS cases. Nonhemophiliacs who had a blood transfusion prior to March 1985 may also become infected with the AIDS virus. Although there have been relatively few cases attributed to transfusion of contaminated blood, there may be more reported in the future since the symptoms of the disease may take many years to show up. Routine screening of blood donations have been in effect since March 1985, and transfusions are now considered safe by most health experts.

Thus far the majority of female victims of the disease have been either intravenous drug users themselves or sexual partners of male drug users. Some health professionals predict that AIDS, which has until now affected primarily the homosexual community, will spread further into the heterosexual population in the future. But changes in certain sexual behaviors, known as "safer sex," can greatly reduce the risk of contracting and spreading AIDS. Safer sex measures include:

▶ Avoidance of sexual contact involving exchange of body fluids (semen, blood, and possibly saliva) with persons who have active AIDS or are AIDS virus carriers.

▶ Sexual monogamy (having only one partner), or greatly limiting the number of sexual partners. Casual sex is considered far riskier than in the past.

▶ Use of condoms (a water-soluble lubricant containing 5 percent nonoxyl-9 may offer additional protection when used with condoms) or diaphragms along with spermicidal jellies, creams, and foams (some evidence suggests that spermicides may help protect against the virus).

▶ Avoidance of unprotected anal intercourse, unprotected oral-genital sexual activity, and deep oral kissing, since cuts or sores in these locations give the AIDS virus access to the bloodstream. The presence of genital herpes triples the risk of infection during sexual relations with an infected partner.

Most cities now have centers and services that can offer testing, information, support, and direct help to those who have AIDS or who test positively for the virus. Information on AIDS is available from a number of organizations, both national and local. Following are some possible sources.

Background Information

The AIDS Epidemic: How You Can Protect Yourself and Your Family—Why You Must by James I. Slaff, M.D., and John K. Brubaker (Warner, 1985).

Medical Answers About AIDS by Lawrence Mass, M.D., a booklet available from Gay Men's Health Crisis, P.O. Box 274, 132 West 24th Street, New York, NY 10011. Send a self-addressed, stamped, business-size envelope.

Answers About AIDS by the American Council on Science and Health. Send a self-addressed, stamped, business-size envelope to AIDS Report, A.C.S.H., 47 Maple Street, Summit, NJ 07901.

A free copy of the brochure "When a Friend Has AIDS . . ." can be obtained by sending a self-addressed, stamped, business-size envelope to Chelsea Psychotherapy Associates, 80 Eighth Avenue, New York, NY 10011.

Coping With AIDS: Psychological and Social Considerations in Helping People With HTLV-III Infection. The National Institute of Mental Health, DHHS Publication No. (ADM) 85-1432, 1986. Single copies can be obtained free of charge from the National Institute of Mental Health, Public Inquiries Branch, 5600 Fishers Lane, Room 15C05, Rockville, MD 20857.

Surgeon General's Report on Acquired Immune Deficiency Syndrome. U.S. Department of Health and Human Services. Washington, DC, 1987.

Telephone Hotlines (toll-free)

> Public Health Service National AIDS Hotline
> (800)342-7514
>
> National Gay Task Force
> AIDS Information Hotline
> (800)221-7044 (outside of New York State)
> (212)529-1604 (New York State)

Information Sources

> U.S. Public Health Service
> Public Affairs Office
> Hubert H. Humphrey Building, Room 725-H
> 200 Independence Avenue, S.W.
> Washington, DC 20201
> (202)245-6867
>
> Local Red Cross or American Red Cross
> AIDS Education Office
> 1730 E Street, N.W.
> Washington, DC 20006
> (202)737-8300

AIDS Action Council
729 Eighth Street, S.E., Suite 200
Washington, DC 20003
(202)547-3101

Gay Men's Health Crisis
P.O. Box 274
132 West 24th Street
New York, NY 10011
(212)807-6655

Hispanic AIDS Forum
140 West 22nd Street, Suite 301
New York, NY 10011
(212)463-8264

Genital Herpes

Caused by a virus known as herpes simplex 2, genital herpes affects five to twenty million Americans, and the incidence is increasing, with 300,000 to 500,000 new cases a year for the past few years. Genital herpes is moderately contagious, usually through sexual contact. It is one of the rare sexually transmitted diseases that can also be contracted through sitting unclothed in an infected place, especially in a warm, moist environment such as hot tubs and whirlpools (although this is uncommon).

Symptoms appear in the form of itching and small, painful "sores" or lesions in the genital area four to seven days after sexual contact. Flu-like symptoms may be present as well as general fatigue. Symptoms often disappear, only to recur. Most people with the active form of the disease have three or four flare-ups a year, each lasting several days to three weeks. The disease is most highly contagious during this time. Women with the disease may be at greater risk for cervical cancer.

If blisters or lesions do occur, they are treated with a cleansing salt solution. Secondary infections may be treated or avoided by use of oral sulfonamides. Though there is currently neither a cure nor a prevention for genital herpes, a new antiviral drug, acyclovir (Zovirax) can prevent flare-ups of the disease, but long-term effects of acyclovir are unknown. Flare-ups may recur if the medication is stopped.

Gonorrhea

It is estimated that close to 3 million people in the United States are infected with gonorrhea annually. Men typically show obvious symptoms two to fourteen days after infection, with a tingling sensation in the urethra, and, shortly thereafter, pain during urination and a discharge from the penis. Some men may be asymptomatic for a period of time. In women, the disease is usually asymptomatic for weeks and even months. When symptoms do occur, they are a vaginal discharge and/or pain on urination, or frequency of urination.

Antibiotics are the usual treatment. Patients are asked to refrain from sexual contact until they are cured, and all recent sexual contacts should be traced and treated as well.

Chlamydia

This may be the most common of all sexually transmitted diseases in the United States. It is often asymptomatic, especially in women. Any onset of unusual vaginal (women) or urethral (men) discharge should be cause for concern. Additional symptoms include pain on urination in men and frequent urination and painful intercourse in women. People experiencing these symptoms should be tested to rule out other sexually transmitted diseases. Once a diagnosis of chlamydia is made, it is easily treated with antibiotics such as tetracycline. If left untreated, chlamydia can cause urethral infections and inflamed testes in men and inflammation of Fallopian tubes in women.

Syphilis

Syphilis is caused by an infectious organism that enters the lymph glands. If untreated, it can unfold over a period of years in three stages, the last of which is a fatal infection of the heart, brain, or other organ. Fortunately, nearly all cases are now detected in the primary stage. Lesions (chancres or "sores") appear about four weeks after infection, or skin rashes in six to eight weeks. Penicillin is the antibiotic treatment of all three stages. Sexual activity must stop during treatment, and all sexual contacts of the preceding three to twelve months should be identified and treated. Retests by the doctor are necessary until all traces of the disease have disappeared.

The early detection and treatment that have been and essentially still are the solution for gonorrhea, syphilis, and most recently chlamydia, are inapplicable to diseases like genital herpes and especially AIDS. The sole protection against such currently incurable diseases is prevention against contracting the disease in the first place. Earlier we outlined recommended sexual behaviors to lessen the risk of exposure to AIDS, especially the avoidance of unprotected intercourse. In the meantime, research efforts must continue to be directed toward learning how to control this dangerous and deadly new public health threat that currently endangers a significant portion of the male population and will perhaps eventually threaten the general population as well.

Chapter 4

The Sexual Effects of Drugs (Including Alcohol) and Surgery

Drugs

Drugs, prescription or otherwise, can and do cause serious sexual problems for both men and women. The impact on sexuality may range from major to subtle effects. Doctors often fail to consider the sexual consequences of drugs they prescribe, and patients are often unaware that the medications they are taking may influence sexual desire or functioning.

Consider your drug use if you are having sexual problems. A study reported in 1983 in the *Journal of the American Medical Association* found that 25 percent of sexual problems in men were either caused or complicated by medications. Less is known about the effects of drugs on female sexuality—but the assumption is that drugs affecting men will affect women as well. Some drugs interfere with the autonomic nervous system, which is involved in normal sexual response. Others affect mood and alertness or change the production or action of sex hormones. (See the tables on pages 61–63).

Prescription Drugs

Tranquilizers, antidepressants, and certain antihypertensives (agents for controlling high blood pressure) have all been impli-

Possible Drug Effects on Female Sexuality

Increased libido: androgens; chlordiazepoxide (*Librium*) (anti-anxiety effect); diazepam (*Valium*) (anti-anxiety effect); mazindol (*Sanorex*).

Decreased libido: (See list of drug effects on male sexuality. Some of these *may* have potential for reducing libido in the female. The literature is sparse on this subject.)

Impaired arousal and orgasm: anticholinergics; clonidine (*Catapres*); methyldopa (*Aldomet*); mono-amine oxidase inhibitors (MAOIs); tricyclic antidepressants (TADs).

Breast enlargement: penicillamine; tricyclic antidepressants (TADs).

Galactorrhea (spontaneous flow of milk): amphetamine; chlorpromazine (*Thorazine*); cimetidine (*Tagamet*); haloperidol (*Haldol*); heroin; methyldopa (*Aldomet*); metoclopramide (*Reglan*); phenothiazines; reserpine (*Serpasil, Ser-Ap-Es*); sulpiride (*Equilid*); tricylic antidepressants (TADs).

Virilization (acne, hirsutism, lowering of voice, enlargement of clitoris): anabolic drugs; androgens; haloperidol (*Haldol*).

Possible Drug Effects on Male Sexuality

Increased libido: androgens (replacement therapy in deficiency states); baclofen (*Lioresal*); chlordiazepoxide (*Librium*) (anti-anxiety effect); diazepam (*Valium*) (anti-anxiety effect); haloperidol (*Haldol*); levodopa (*Larodopa, Sinemet*) (may be an indirect effect due to improved sense of well-being).

Decreased libido: antihistamines; barbiturates; chlordiazepoxide (*Librium*) (sedative effect); chlorpromazine (*Thorazine*) 10–20% of users; cimetidine (*Tagamet*); clofibrate (*Atromid-S*); clonidine (*Catapres*) 10–20% of users; diazepam (*Valium*) (sedative effect); disulfiram (*Antabuse*); estrogens (therapy for prostatic cancer); fenfluramine (*Pondimin*); heroin; licorice; medroxyprogesterone (*Provera*); methyldopa (*Aldomet*)10–15% of users; perhexilene (*Pexid*); prazosin (*Minipress*) 15% of users; propranolol (*Inderal*) rarely; reserpine (*Serpasil, Ser-Ap-Es*); spironolactone (*Aldactone*); tricyclic antidepressants (TADs).

(continued)

Impaired erection (impotence): anticholinergics; antihistamines; baclofen (*Lioresal*); barbiturates (when abused); chlordiazepoxide (*Librium*) (in high dosage); chlorpromazine (*Thorazine*); cimetidine (*Tagamet*); clofibrate (*Atromid-S*); clonidine (*Catapres*) 10–20% of users; cocaine; diazepam (*Valium*) (in high dosage); digitalis and its glycosides; disopyramide (*Norpace*); disulfiram (*Antabuse*) (uncertain); estrogens (therapy for prostatic cancer); ethacrynic acid (*Edecrin*) 5% of users; ethionamide (*Trecator-SC*); fenfluramine (*Pondimin*); furosemide (*Lasix*) 5% of users; guanethidine (*Ismelin*); haloperidol (*Haldol*) 10–20% of users; heroin; hydroxyprogesterone (therapy for prostatic cancer); licorice; lithium (*Lithonate*); marijuana; mesoridazine (*Serentil*); methantheline (*Banthine*); methyldopa (*Aldomet*) 10–15% of users; mono-amine oxidase inhibitors (MAOIs) 10–15% of users; perhexilene (*Pexid*); prazosin (*Minipress*) infrequently; propranolol (*Inderal*) infrequently; reserpine (*Serpasil, Ser-Ap-Es*); spironolactone (*Aldactone*); thiazide diuretics 5% of users; thioridazine (*Mellaril*); tricyclic antidepressants (TADs).

Impaired ejaculation: anticholinergics; barbiturates (when abused); chlorpromazine (*Thorazine*); clonidine (*Catapres*); estrogens (therapy for prostatic cancer); guanethidine (*Ismelin*); heroin; mesoridazine (*Serentil*); methyldopa (*Aldomet*); mono-amine oxidase inhibitors (MAOIs); phenoxybenzamine (*Dibenzyline*); phentolamine (*Regitine*); reserpine (*Serpasil, Ser-Ap-Es*); thiazide diuretics; thioridazine (*Mellaril*); tricyclic antidepressants (TADs).

Decreased plasma testosterone: adrenocorticotropic hormone (ACTH); barbiturates; digoxin (*Lanoxin*); haloperidol (*Haldol*) (increased testosterone with low dosage, decreased testosterone with high dosage); lithium (*Lithonate*); marijuana; medroxyprogesterone (*Provera*); mono-amine oxidase inhibitors (MAOIs); spironolactone (*Aldactone*).

Impaired spermatogenesis (reduced fertility): adrenocorticosteroids (prednisone, etc.); androgens (moderate to high dosage, extended use); antimalarials; aspirin (abusive, chronic use); chlorambucil (*Leukeran*); cimetidine (*Tagamet*); colchicine; co-trimoxazole (*Bactrim, Septra*); cyclophosphamide (*Cytoxan*); estrogens (therapy for prostatic cancer); marijuana; medroxyprogesterone (*Provera*); methotrexate; mono-amine oxidase inhibitors (MAOIs); niridazole (*Ambilhar*); nitrofurantoin (*Furadantin*); spironolactone (*Aldactone*); sulfasalazine (*Azulfidine*); testosterone (moderate to high dosage, extended use); vitamin C (in doses of 1 gram or more).

Testicular disorders:
Swelling: tricyclic antidepressants (TADs). **Inflammation:**
oxyphenbutazone (*Tandearil*). **Atrophy:** androgens (moderate to high
dosage, extended use); chlorpromazine (*Thorazine*); spironolactone
(*Aldactone*).

Penile disorders:
Priapism: cocaine; heparin; phenothiazines. **Peyronie's disease:**
metoprolol (*Lopressor*).

Gynecomastia (excessive development of the male breast):
androgens (partial conversion to estrogen); BCNU; busulfan
(*Myleran*); chlormadinone; chlorpromazine (*Thorazine*);
chlortetracycline (*Aureomycin*) cimetidine (*Tagamet*); clonidine
(*Catapres*) infrequently; diethylstilbestrol (DES); digitalis and its
glycosides; estrogens (therapy for prostatic cancer); ethionamide
(*Trecator-SC*); griseofulvin (*Fulvicin*, etc.); haloperidol (*Haldol*);
heroin; isoniazid (*INH, Nydrazid*); marijuana; methyldopa (*Aldomet*);
phenelzine (*Nardil*); reserpine (*Serpasil, Ser-Ap-Es*); spironolactone
(*Aldactone*); thioridazine (*Mellaril*); tricyclic antidepressants (TADs);
vincristine (*Oncovin*).

**Feminization (loss of libido, impotence, gynecomastia,
testicular atrophy):** conjugated estrogens (*Premarin*, etc.).

Tables reprinted from "Many Common Medications Can Affect Sexual Expression" by James W. Long, M.D., Generations VI (1981).

cated in impaired erection in men. Effects on women are less
well understood.

Tranquilizers. Strong tranquilizers such as Mellaril (thioridazine) and other phenothiazines may cause failure to obtain an
erection or to ejaculate even when the capacity for erection remains. Any tranquilizing drug, even a mild one such as Librium
(chlordiazepoxide), can also act as a depressant on the sexual
feelings of both women and men.

Antidepressants. Antidepressants such as imipramine hydrochloride (Tofranil) also inhibit sexual desire. According to two
reports in the February 1985 *Journal of Clinical Psychopharma-*

cology, adverse sexual side effects have been reported with all standard antidepressants.

Antihypertensives. Antihypertensive medications are the most common cause of impaired erection. "Blocking agents," one class of antihypertensive drugs, include methyldopa (Aldomet), which reduces the flow of blood into the pelvic area and so inhibits erection of the penis. Another drug used against hypertension, guanethidine (Ismelin), may inhibit ejaculation by blocking the nerves involved. Up to two-thirds of men taking the medication have reported problems. Guanethidine can also cause retrograde ejaculation (see page 78). The common antihypertensive reserpine can decrease sexual interest or, at times, induce impotence. Even the diuretics given for high blood pressure can cause problems.

Patients who develop sexual problems after taking antihypertensive medications may be tempted to discontinue or decrease medication without telling their doctor. This can be very dangerous, since the medication could be preventing a stroke. Remember that your doctor may be able to help without putting your life in danger. Some alternatives are to switch antihypertensives, to use only a diuretic, and/or to reduce dosages when feasible. Many physicians no longer prescribe medications for mild to moderate hypertension until patients have first tried to bring blood pressure under control by lowering salt intake and by exercise and weight reduction. When drugs are necessary, one study suggests that one of the most effective regimens, with the least likelihood of sexual impairment, is a combination of an oral diuretic, hydralazine, and propranolol. However, propranolol, promoted at first for its lack of sexual side effects, has now been implicated as affecting sexuality, especially when higher dosages are used.

Other Drugs. The corticosteroids taken for arthritis may produce at least temporary impotence. Analgesics (pain medications) may reduce sensitivity and therefore affect male sexual capacity. Cimetidine (Tagamet), used in the treatment of duodenal ulcers and one of the most widely sold medicines in the United States, can cause impotence. Ranitidine (Zantac) is a possible substitute for cimetidine.

Alcohol

Most people do not realize that alcohol is a drug. Pharmacologically it is a depressant rather than a stimulant, though in small amounts it may relax sexual inhibition in a pleasant manner. In larger amounts, however, it usually interferes with sexual performance, reducing potency in males and orgasmic ability in females. At the very least, alcohol often produces drowsiness, which then interferes with sex. The excessive use of alcohol is a frequent and too-little-recognized factor in sexual problems, and often those who abuse alcohol fail to realize how much they are actually drinking.

Even a few drinks before sex can affect a man's sexual performance. Erections may be less firm and ejaculation more difficult. But though this effect is temporary and reversible in terms of physical capacity, it can frighten a man into believing he is impotent, and fear itself may prolong the impotence.

Up to 80 percent of men who drink heavily are believed to have serious sexual side effects, including impotence, sterility, or loss of sexual desire. Many of the effects of moderate to heavy drinking may be reversible if drinking stops in time. However, heavy drinking over a long period irreversibly destroys testicular cells, leaving men with shrunken testicles. Both sexual drive and sexual capacity can be damaged. Hormone production is often affected, resulting in a decrease in testosterone and a drop in the sperm count. Total sterility as well as impotence result. Chronic heavy drinking can also produce liver and brain damage that leads to excess production of female hormones and a feminized body appearance.

Women are affected by alcohol in many of the same ways as men. More than one drink before a sexual encounter can interfere with the ability to reach orgasm. Chronic heavy use of alcohol in the middle years can damage the ovaries, causing menstrual and ovulatory abnormalities and a decrease in estrogen production. This in turn may lead to early menopause and signs of premature aging. Atrophy of the breasts, uterus, and vaginal walls and lessened lubrication in the vagina are common.

Tolerance for alcohol decreases with age (one cause is changing kidney excretory power), so that smaller and smaller amounts may begin to produce negative effects. It is wise to avoid drinking altogether for several hours before a sexual encounter, or at least to limit alcohol to one drink. Persons who choose to drink regularly should limit themselves to a maximum of one and a half ounces of hard liquor, one six-ounce glass of wine, or two eight-ounce glasses of beer in any twenty-four-hour period. Remember, too, that alcohol is very dangerous in combination with narcotic and non-narcotic drugs such as sleeping pills, sedatives, painkillers, antihistamines, antidepressants, and tranquilizers, because it can pyramid their effects. If you are taking drugs, do not drink without discussing it with your doctor.

Tobacco

Because of its nicotine content, tobacco is also a drug, although not usually categorized as one. It may be a factor in impotence. There is an old German saying about male erectile capacity: *"Rauchen macht schlump"*—"Smoking makes [it] dangle." Toxic changes in the blood from nicotine may affect sex hormones. There is some evidence that men who smoke have lower levels of testosterone. Nicotine also constricts blood vessels, in some cases enough to affect blood flow to the penis. Long-term smokers with atherosclerosis or peripheral vascular disease can become impotent.

Narcotics and Other Drugs

Regular users of opiates like morphine and heroin are often sexually impaired. Males who are addicted are usually impotent.

Cocaine use is growing, as cocaine has become more readily available at lower prices. A primary attraction of cocaine is that initially it heightens sexual sensation in both men and women as a result of euphoria, increased energy, and heightened self-confidence. With habitual use, however, individuals experience a lowered sense of self-esteem, together with insomnia, fatigue, anxiety, depression, and even paranoia, hallucinations, and seizures. Women become nonorgasmic and men impotent. A national telephone aid line—800-COCAINE—has been established for those who want help in stopping cocaine use.

Marijuana can lead to decreased sexual interest and impotence as well as drying of the mucous membranes in the sex organs. Amphetamines can produce impotence, delayed or no ejaculation in men, and inhibition of orgasms in women. Regular users of such barbiturates as sedatives and hypnotics (sleeping pills) may become impotent.

A rare but exceedingly destructive condition called priapism can occur in men who use certain drugs such as butyl (or isobutyl) nitrate, known also as "poppers," to stimulate more frequent and longer-lasting erections. An antidepressant drug, trazodone (Desyrel), can also cause similar problems. Priapism is a persistent and often painful erection of the penis caused by blood becoming trapped in the corpora cavernosa—the chambers in the penis that fill with blood to create erections. The erection does not subside, and emergency medical care is needed within twenty-four hours or less to avoid permanent damage to the penis and almost certain permanent impotence. Partial priapism —any unusual period of persistent erection which eventually goes away by itself—is a sign that something is wrong and medical advice and treatment are indicated.

Avoiding Problems

Health care professionals who prescribe or monitor the use of drugs should be thoroughly familiar with each drug's potential for adverse effects on sexuality. (Dr. James W. Long's annually updated book *The Essential Guide to Prescription Drugs* [Harper & Row] is a useful reference.) It is also important to obtain a patient's sexual history before giving any drug that may affect sexuality. This allows comparisons to be made before and after drugs are taken. A patient's drug usage should be reviewed regularly, including prescription and other over-the-counter drugs, alcohol, and tobacco. Doctors should carefully explain the potential side effects of drugs.

Most drug-caused sexual impairment is reversible if the responsible drug is reduced, removed, or replaced by another. (Impairment due to chronic alcoholism and possibly marijuana use may *not* be reversible.) In cases of serious illness, obviously, sexuality may have to be partially or even totally sacrificed for a period of time in order to obtain the beneficial effects of drugs that are essential to treatment. But in many cases, alternative drugs, lower dosages, or other treatment altogether can be given. For example, an antihypertensive drug that may adversely affect one person's sexuality will not affect another's. The possible sexual side effects of a drug must be balanced against the risks of a disease, with the patient's preference a crucial factor in the decision.

Surgery

It's not surprising that people are apprehensive about surgery on their sex organs. They dread possible sexual consequences in addition to the usual risks involved in any surgical procedure. Women commonly believe removal of the womb (hysterectomy) or of a breast (mastectomy) makes them "less of a woman." Men worry that prostate surgery means the end of sex life altogether. It is reassuring to know that the medical evidence does not support many of these fears, as long as surgeons are skilled, knowledgeable about the possible problems, and sensitive to patients' interest in preserving sexual functioning.

Hysterectomy

A hysterectomy is the removal of the womb or uterus. In addition, the ovaries and Fallopian tubes may also be removed (bilateral salpingo-ovariectomy). It is estimated that more than half of all women will have had a hysterectomy by age sixty-five, making this the most common major operation performed in the United States; twice as many hysterectomies are performed in this country as in England or Sweden. Evidence is growing that some of these operations are unnecessary, such as those performed to prevent cancer of the ovaries and uterus. A second or third opinion about the need for surgery is strongly suggested. HERS (Hysterectomy Educational Resources and Services) offers counseling and support to women and their families faced with the question of surgery. Write 422 Bryn Mawr Avenue, Bala Cynwyd, PA 19004.

Many hysterectomies are done because of the presence of benign (noncancerous) tumors called fibroids, which are not troublesome so long as they remain small but may require surgery if they enlarge, cause bleeding, or involve other organs. Prolapse of the uterus ("fallen uterus"); cancer of the cervix, the endometrium (lining of the uterus), or related organs; and severe, uncontrollable infection or bleeding are other legitimate reasons for a hysterectomy.

It is often said there is no medical evidence that careful removal of the uterus causes impairment of sexual sensations. Yet some women greatly depend on sensations from the cervix and womb to achieve orgasm through deep penile penetration and must learn after hysterectomy other methods of arousal, such as more focus on clitoral stimulation. The rhythmic contractions of the uterus during orgasm are of course gone as a result of a hysterectomy. During the surgical repair, surgeons are not always careful to avoid shortening the vagina, which can lead to problems with intercourse. Correct positioning of the wound repair in the back of the vagina is also important. If intercourse is resumed too early after hysterectomy, there can be pain due to incomplete healing in the vagina. Most physicians recommend waiting six to eight weeks before sexual activity is begun again.

Many surgeons and women themselves warn that a period of emotional instability commonly begins about the third or fourth day after a hysterectomy and lasts two to five or ten days or longer. Depression, sleep disturbances, fatigue, listlessness, weight gain, loss of appetite, weeping, and irritability may occur —physical and/or emotional responses to the surgery. Rarely are they severe or long lasting enough to require psychotherapeutic care. Most women regain their equilibrium naturally, although many claim that it takes six months or longer to fully recover physically, especially if the ovaries have been removed. *Coping with Hysterectomy* by Suzanne Morgan (Dial Press, 1982) is a useful guide for dealing with the issues surrounding hysterectomy.

Removal of all or parts of a woman's childbearing apparatus, powerful symbols of womanhood, often does have significant psychological effects. If the woman sees the surgery as symbolic "castration," she needs to resolve this, either on her own or with outside help. She must understand that removal of the sexual organs need not eradicate sexuality, cause her to feel unattractive, or diminish her womanliness. Short-term preoperative and postoperative counseling, ideally with her partner present, can do much to allay a woman's fears and misapprehensions. Group discussions with other women who have had hysterectomies can be especially helpful. Women's health centers or hospital social workers may be able to arrange this.

Hysterectomies can have positive effects on sexuality, particularly if they are done to relieve painful or debilitating conditions like infection, urinary incontinence, heavy bleeding, or endometriosis. A return to pain-free good health can be a potent aphrodisiac.

Mastectomy

While most breast lumps (80 to 90 percent) are found to be benign upon biopsy, unfortunately the likelihood of breast cancer increases with age. Full or partial breast removal, or mastectomy, is performed when a lump in the breast is found to be malignant (cancerous).

In spite of current controversy over whether breast cancer

begins in the breast or is a systemic disease beginning else-where, most physicians emphasize early detection of lumps as a major means of combating the disease. In addition to routine examination by your physician and the use of newer techniques to help him or her in diagnosis (for example, mammography by low-voltage X rays), you should undertake regular monthly self-examinations. We recommend *The Breast Cancer Digest: A Guide to Medical Care, Emotional Support, Educational Programs and Resources* (Office of Cancer Communications, National Cancer Institute, Bethesda, MD 20003, 1984). Recent results of a large study in Sweden on women between the ages of forty and seventy-four show that regular mammograms cut death rates from cancer by almost one-third.

There are different kinds of mastectomy, ranging from removal of the lump(s) and some adjacent tissue only to the removal of the entire breast, the surrounding lymph glands, and chest muscles. These operations have understandable psychological implications for many women, because they not only change the outward appearance of the body but visibly alter a specific symbol of sexuality. Periodic depression, with consequences for one's sex life, is common and expected during the first year or two after a mastectomy. Aesthetic reactions to breast removal can be more difficult than with a hysterectomy, which leaves no obvious signs beyond an abdominal scar.

Although there is no physiological change in sexual capacity after mastectomy, women may temporarily lose their sexual desire out of embarrassment, inability to accept the loss of the breast, and fear that they have become less attractive to their sexual partners. They are afraid the absence of the breast will be noticeable in public. A properly fitting prosthetic bra can relieve worries about public appearance, but reactions to breast loss by women themselves and their partners are not always so easily resolved. One useful technique is for women to talk frankly with other women who have already experienced a breast loss. Some physicians and hospitals arrange for such volunteers to counsel women prior to and following surgery. The Reach to

Recovery program of the American Cancer Society, begun by Terese Lazar in 1952, is a rehabilitation program for women who have had breast surgery. (A helpful free booklet, "Reach to Recovery," is available from local units of the American Cancer Society.) The program is designed to help with physical, psychological, and cosmetic concerns, and utilizes a carefully selected and trained corps of volunteers who have adjusted successfully to their own surgery. Other forms of individual and group support can be immensely relieving as well.

Men, too, need a period of adjustment to work out their feelings about breast surgery in their partners. In some cities, Reach to Recovery uses male volunteers to help men adjust to their wives' mastectomies. In sturdy relationships, time and affection often take care of disturbed feelings following breast removal. Severe and prolonged emotional upset may require professional psychotherapy. Do not avoid seeking aid in such cases; the odds are that it will help greatly, whether the problem is with you or with your mate.

Specific recommendations that may speed the resumption of a normal sex life include:

▶ Involving the partner in all aspects of the discussions around a mastectomy.
▶ Having the partner see the wound as early as possible after surgery, so the process of adjustment can begin.
▶ Resuming sexual activity as soon as possible.
▶ Finding sexual positions that will be comfortable. For the first weeks and months, the patient's wound will be sensitive. A preferred sexual position is to have the partner on top, supporting his upper body with his arms. This leaves the woman in a relaxed position on her back, with no stress on her chest area.
▶ Deciding together whether the woman wants to wear a prosthesis (a padded bra) during sexual contact or whether the couple can be comfortable without it. Many couples eventually eliminate the need for the cover-up.

▶ Sharing feeings openly and supporting each other emotionally. Both partners are likely to have periods of depression and anxiety due to the fear of death that cancer brings and to reactions to the loss of a valued body part. Couples who can share such feelings may not need further counseling after the initial adjustment period.

Breast cancer treatment today is highly controversial. A few years ago most surgeons performed what is called the Halsted radical mastectomy, removing the entire breast, underlying muscles, and the nearby lymph nodes. This left a woman with a sunken chest wall and impaired mobility of the arm. When it was discovered that surgeons in countries such as Canada and England were removing much less breast tissue and getting nearly identical survival rates, American surgeons began changing their approach. Most now do the modified radical mastectomy, which removes less muscle and fewer lymph nodes. This operation is less disfiguring. The remaining question is whether mastectomies are any more effective than lumpectomies (removal of the lump) combined with radiation. Further evidence is needed, although figures from Canada and Europe would suggest that the simpler, less invasive procedure may have equivalent survival rates.

Vaginal Reconstruction

Women who have had a number of children, difficult childbirths, or tears in the opening of the vagina at the time of childbirth may have an excessively enlarged vagina. Anterior and posterior plastic repair, a surgical procedure, may reconstruct the vagina effectively and make sex more pleasurable. This is a delicate operation and requires an especially skilled surgeon who is also sensitive to the woman's needs. A second medical opinion on the advisability of surgery is recommended.

Prostatectomy

Prostatectomy involves surgical removal of part or all of the prostate, a gland located at the base of the urethra. As men grow older, up to half of them experience significant enlargement of the prostate. This usually begins after age forty or fifty, and almost all men over fifty have some degree of enlargement. Fifty to 75 percent have noticeable symptoms and at least half eventually require surgery. By age eighty prostate problems are almost universal, although in a few cases the prostate gland atrophies with extreme age. No one knows yet why the prostate undergoes growth in midlife after a period of dormancy following adolescence. There is evidence that black men develop prostate enlargement an average of five years earlier than white men. There also appear to be lower rates of enlargement among non-American Asian men compared to American Asian men. Diet may be a factor, especially large amounts of fat. Some physicians believe a zinc deficiency may be involved, but there is no solid evidence for this. Zinc taken in small doses will do no harm, but it is not a medically proved treatment or preventive for prostate problems. When the enlargement is noncancerous, as is usually the case, it is called benign prostatic hyperplasia (too many cells), or BPH. BPH starts very gradually and may exist for years with no symptoms. In fact, many men remain symptomless throughout their lives except for the enlargement. A reliable and readable book for men and their partners is *What Every Man Should Know About His Prostate* by Monroe Greenburger, M.D., and Mary-Ellen Siegel, M.S.W. (Walker and Company, 1983).

The size of the enlarged gland is less significant than the amount of obstruction it produces at the neck of the bladder. Since the prostate gland is so close to the bladder and urethra, enlargement can produce problems with urination. Men may find themselves with some or all of the following symptoms: An enlarged prostate may increase the need and urgency to urinate or to get up to void during the night. There may be a delay in starting the stream of urine, a slowness or weakness in the stream, or even a total inability to urinate. Occasionally, small amounts of blood are present in the urine and during ejaculation. (Bleeding should always be medically evaluated, since it could also be a symptom of cancer.) The dribbling of urine after urination is common, requiring the use of paper tissues for a few minutes to catch the drops of urine. Since enlargement of the gland may lead to retention and stagnation of urine, there can be bacterial infection. In severe and untreated cases, damage is done to the kidneys. Surgery is absolutely necessary when a urinary shutdown occurs.

The causes of noncancerous prostatic difficulties are unknown but may be connected to genetics, to changes in endocrine levels, and/or to the aging process itself. Previous theories about changes in hormone levels seem to have been disproved at Johns Hopkins Medical School and elsewhere. A curious aspect of BPH is that it has been found in aging men and aging dogs, but in no other species. There is no foundation to the folklore that prostate trouble is related to "excessive" sexual activity. Indeed, evidence suggests that an active and regular sex life preserves healthy prostate functioning, while a pattern of irregular ejaculations may lead to problems such as inflammation.

Cancer of the prostate, a much more serious disorder, occurs largely in men over sixty. The cause is still unknown. It does not appear that men with BPH have higher rates of prostate cancer than those without BPH. Most such cancers are not detected until men are in their seventies, and cancer of the prostate is the second leading cause of cancer deaths in men, killing 25,500 annually. The probability of developing prostate cancer in one's lifetime is about 9 percent for American men. However, if detected early, many cases can be successfully treated with surgery and radiation. The cancer is relatively slow-growing and may go through dormant periods. A physical exam at least once a year after age forty, including a digital (finger) rectal examination and a complete urinalysis, greatly enhances the chance of early detection.

A new technique using an ultrasound probe in the rectum to

study the entire prostate has been developed in Japan. It is still under experimental study at the Preventive Medicine Institute–Strang Clinic in New York, and elsewhere.

Advances in the medical (probably hormonal) treatment of benign prostatic hypertrophy seem promising but are not yet of practical use. A new treatment using a laser is currently being tested. The YAG laser is an intense light beam that can be used under local anesthesia to destroy the excess prostate tissue in benign prostatic enlargement. The tissue is then voided with the urine. The advantage of the laser is that it avoids other surgical procedures and allows the extra tissue to be painlessly eliminated. This is still experimental, however, and not yet available for the general public. Surgery remains the treatment of choice. Some doctors now recommend surgery at an earlier point in the course of symptoms to avoid unnecessary complications and dire emergencies; the decision is made by patient and doctor.

There are three types of prostate surgery, all requiring anesthesia:

Transurethral resection, or TUR, is the commonest, least traumatic, and safest procedure because it requires no outside incision. A thin, hollow, fiber-optic tube is inserted in the penis, an electric loop is maneuvered through the tube, and the gland is removed. One disadvantage of this technique is that the tissue sometimes grows back. TUR is recommended chiefly when the prostate is not too enlarged, and for men over seventy.

Suprapubic or *retropubic* surgery (named for the site of the incision, above or behind the pubic bone) is performed when the gland is very large. The tissue is removed through an incision made in the abdomen.

Perineal surgery is used by some surgeons for men with substantial prostate enlargement who are in poor physical condition. There is very little postoperative bleeding or pain with this procedure. An even more radical perineal procedure is used in the surgical treatment of cancer of the gland. These procedures can be performed with a high degree of safety even on a very elderly man. An incision is made in the perineum between the scrotum and the anus, and most or all of the prostate is removed. Whether surgery is more effective than radiotherapy for operable prostate cancer is questioned. Radiotherapy, however, results in impotence in only about 50 percent of men, compared to the nearly 100 percent impotence caused by perineal surgery.

Potency is rarely affected by the TUR and suprapubic procedures, and some men experience increased potency because their prostatic problems have been eliminated. It is generally agreed that 80 percent of men return to their presurgery sexual functioning, 10 percent have improved sexual functioning, while 10 percent have some or even total loss of the ability to achieve an erection. The perineal approach—especially the radical procedure—has been the chief physical cause of impotence following prostatic surgery because critical nerves are cut. Perineal surgery also may affect the ability to urinate by causing strictures to form in the urethra. Dilation of the urethra is then required.

Freezing Technique. For prostate cancer, a freezing technique, rather than gland removal, is being tested by urologist Maurice Gonder at the State University of New York at Stony Brook. This cryosurgery, used more widely in Europe, destroys the tumor cells and stimulates the body to produce an immune response against the tumor.

Nerve-Sparing Surgery. In 1982 a "nerve-sparing operation" (a modified radical retropubic prostatectomy), designed to protect the nerve centers damaged by the usual cancer surgery, was developed at Johns Hopkins by Dr. Patrick Walsh. A number of clinics now offer such surgery, which preserves potency in 70–90 percent of men who have the operation.

Prior to surgery, prostate problems usually do not interfere with sexual functioning unless pain is present. Some men may experience a slight decrease in the force of their ejaculation, but others may have benign prostate problems for years with no change in sexual functioning. After a prostatectomy, as we have noted, most men return to normal sexual activity. Healing time runs at least six weeks, and most men wait four to six weeks before resuming sexual activity. The only change after most types of surgery is that in many cases semen is no longer ejaculated through the penis but instead is pushed backward into the bladder (retrograde ejaculation), where it is voided with the urine. This so-called dry ejaculation happens because a space has been left where the enlarged prostate had been, and fluid travels the path of least resistance to the bladder. Although men in this situation can no longer father children, the large majority have erections as before, with no diminishment of sexual pleasure. (However, if couples wish, sperm can be successfully extracted from the urine and deposited in the younger female partner's vagina for fertilization purposes.) Couples should not depend on retrograde ejaculation for birth control, since some semen may pass down through the penis. In addition, normal ejaculation may return following some regrowth of the prostate; in such instances, fertility may be restored. A certain amount of regrowth can occur without causing difficulties before surgery is again, if ever, necessary.

By far the greatest cause of impotence occurring with prostatectomies is *psychological*. Unfortunately, family doctors and urologists do not always give a man adequate information about what to expect after surgery, so that he falsely assumes sexual impairment. This assumption, with its consequent fear, is based on the tendency to associate the prostate gland with the penis, since men know the two are in physical proximity.

Beware of the many quack remedies that promise treatment without surgery. Various kinds of massage, foods, and other "cures," often at exorbitant prices, are offered to men seeking a quick cure for a sometimes serious condition. Avoid them and rely on your physician's advice.

Orchidectomy

This surgery, removal of the testes, may follow cancer of the prostate. The psychological impact of this castration can be devastating. Emotional preparation before and counseling following surgery are indispensable. The creation of artificial testes of plastic or tantalum may be advisable for cosmetic and emotional reasons. Impotence does not always follow removal of the testes; some men continue with normal erections.

Colostomy and Ileostomy

When part of the bowel must be removed for lifesaving purposes, the anus is generally closed and an artificial opening in the abdomen created. The surgery may be in the colon (colostomy) or in the ileum (an ileostomy). Needless to say, the patient has many sensitive adjustments to make after such surgery. A bag attached to the opening fills with feces and must be emptied, although many colostomy patients develop enough bowel predictability to simply wear a gauze pad. There are possible embarrassing bowel sounds as well as odors. Much of this can be controlled adequately. Patients have to work their way through their own feelings, however, as well as their perceptions of other people's attitudes. The most complicated issue of all can be the working out of the sexual relationship with one's partner. Information specific to ostomies, and perhaps counseling, can help greatly.

Estimates are that it may take up to a year to make a full and relatively comfortable adjustment to an ostomy. The patient's primary physician as well as the surgeon is central in helping patients anticipate and circumvent or resolve problems. Although most people are grateful that their lives have been spared by ostomies, it is normal to experience difficulties in accepting the changes in one's body. Patients who had active sex lives prior to ostomies usually continue to have them afterward, but inevitably there is a complex adjustment process, and patients and their partners should not hesitate to seek help. Over a million people in the United States have had ostomies, and United Ostomy Clubs have been formed, which can offer a great deal of help. For information on the local chapter nearest you (there are more than 250 nationwide), contact the United Ostomy Association, 2001 West Beverly Boulevard, Los Angeles, CA 90057. "Sex,

Courtship and the Single Ostomate" is a pamphlet available from the association.

Rectal Cancer Surgery

If a cancerous tumor is operable and is not in the lower two-thirds of the rectum, surgery can be done that not only permits normal bowel function but also allows normal sexual activity. However, if removal of the tumor requires removal of the rectum and anus, with a permanent colostomy, men may become totally impotent. The closeness of male genital organs to the lower rectum leaves essential nerve fibers vulnerable to damage from such surgery. Women, though, maintain capacity for sexual arousal and orgasm even after rectal surgery, since the essential nerves involved are farther removed from the surgical site.

In general, for both men and women, the emotionally charged aspects of surgery and its effects on sexuality can be relatively short-lived if people spell out their fears and if their misconceptions are cleared up. Unfortunately, they often do not get the opportunity to do this. Doctors do not always take the time to explain procedures and answer questions, though counseling before surgery is extremely helpful in preventing anxiety and clarifying misunderstandings. After the operation, continued advice and emotional support from medical personnel, family and friends, and special organizations are crucial to adjustment. Be sure to ask for help, and if you remain troubled, seek professional psychotherapy to work through more complicated feelings.

Even under the best of modern techniques, rates of recovery vary with the individual after surgery of any kind. Some people find their stamina or vitality reduced for some time, even though healing has been satisfactory. Surgeons do not always make it clear to their patients that these are normal variations. You have no reason to worry if this happens to you, as long as your surgeon has assured you that your postoperative recovery is progressing as it should be. Once you are feeling entirely well again, your level of sexual activity is likely to return to normal.

Chapter 5

Sexual Fitness

S ex is one of the great free and renewable pleasures of life. To get the most out of it, you will do yourself a favor if you are in shape for it. Two powerful aphrodisiacs are a vigorous and well-cared-for body and a lively personality. Much can be done to preserve the functioning of both, though we shall be talking here specifically about your body. The overall formula for keeping in good health and preventing a multitude of problems is a simple one: no smoking, moderate use of alcohol, control of blood pressure and weight, balanced nutrition, regular exercise, and adequate rest.

Fitness for Older People

The enjoyment of sex is enhanced by a fairly healthy, fairly pain-free body. Apart from visits to the doctor for a specific complaint, older men and women ideally should have a physical examination every year. Women should also have a gynecological examination every six months, particularly to check for breast and vaginal cancer. Any problems in sexual functioning should be brought to the doctor's attention at the time of these examinations, if not at a special appointment in between. The purpose of all this is to detect and treat physical problems in their early stages and to provide medical guidance for a program of preventive health care, including exercise, nutrition, and rest.

Exercise

Exercise can improve physical appearance and increase longevity. It is crucial for a healthy heart, arteries, and respiratory system and has a relaxing effect on the nervous system. Studies indicate that bones maintain their size and strength better during aging if one exercises regularly. In addition, exercise can improve one's sex life. The only bad news is that it requires discipline and a certain amount of work. Although we are improving our habits as a nation, many Americans do not exercise at all, and older people exercise less than younger people do. This is unfortunate, since the older you are, the more help your body needs from you. Exercise should be planned on a routine and daily basis.

Physical fitness is a quality of life, a condition of looking and feeling well and having the necessary physical reserves to enjoy a range of interests, including sex. Fitness has two components. Basic health or *organic fitness* means a well-nourished body as free as possible from disease or infirmity, with physical limitations compensated for to the greatest degree possible. The second component, *dynamic fitness,* means not simply freedom from disease but full ability to move vigorously and energetically. This involves efficiency of heart and lungs, muscular strength and endurance, balance, flexibility, coordination, and agility.

Two distinct kinds of exercise are necessary: one to keep the body limber and supple and strengthen the muscles (stretching and flexing exercises), the other to increase endurance and enlarge the heart capacity (aerobic exercises).

To achieve fitness, you should exercise aerobically at least twenty to thirty minutes three to five times a week, at about 70 percent of your age-adjusted maximum heart rate. To find the maximum rate, subtract your age from 220. For example, a sixty-year-old would subtract 60 from 220, which is 160. Seventy percent of 160 would equal 112 heartbeats a minute, or about 18 beats every ten seconds. For aerobic benefit, fast walking, swimming, cycling, cross-country skiing, and skating, all of which involve continual movement, are better than basketball, dance, handball, tennis, and racquetball, which involve intermittent movement. Jogging and fast action sports like racquetball frequently cause injury to the bones and joints.

Brisk walking is perhaps the best all-around exercise for older people, accompanied by a regimen of calisthenics. The squeezing action of the leg muscles on the veins during walking helps promote the return of blood to the heart. Start out by walking rapidly until you begin to feel tired. Rest and walk back to your starting point. Keep doing this for progressively longer distances until you reach a reasonable goal, such as a walk of two to three miles a day in forty-five minutes. This may take a year or so if you have previously been sedentary.

As a supplement to a regular program of exercise, older people should take advantage of any opportunity for physical movement—walking upstairs, doing chores, mowing the lawn, gardening—in short, bending, stretching, and moving as much as possible.

If you have been unusually inactive or had any indication of possible heart disease, take a treadmill stress test (available in most hospitals) before jogging, swimming, and other more vigorous activities. Swimming is particularly useful for anyone with a joint disease like arthritis or orthopedic problems such as damaged knees or chronic backache. It is not recommended as the major physical activity to protect against osteoporosis, however, because it is not weight-bearing on the long bones of the body.

The use of a stationary bicycle is popular with older people because it has the advantage of being available in all kinds of weather, and, if you have one in your home, requires no transportation to and from exercise periods. It also allows accurate measurement of the amount of exercise you are getting. However, you must have good knees, no major orthopedic problems, and be strongly motivated to exercise alone, if you use a bicycle at home.

Spa fitness centers, exercise resorts, and the best of the aerobic centers and health clubs that are proliferating in and near major cities have begun to pay more attention to the medical as well as the aesthetic and social aspects of exercise. Most are coed, and men must be warned that they will not usually be able to achieve the same level of flexibility as most women. This is not a sign that they are not trying hard enough. It simply means that male and female bodies are different, and women are by nature more flexible. On the other hand, men often have a natural advantage over women in exercises that emphasize strength. Ideally, both men and women should approach exercise noncompetitively. In fact, because there are wide variations in physical performance and capacity your own individual physical condition should determine your appropriate exercise and its level and pace. If you become temporarily ill or inactive, you will usually need to return to an earlier level of activity and slowly work your way up. In all cases, avoid strenuous bursts of sudden activity when you are out of shape. It is recommended that you discuss your exercise program with your own doctor and ask him or her to advise you.

Some people don't exercise out of the fear that it will provoke a heart attack. But exercise opposes the effect of stroke or heart attack. Blood clots form when the blood is sluggish rather than when it is circulating vigorously. A study of 17,000 middle-aged and older Harvard alumni over several years by Dr. Ralph Paffenbarger and colleagues, published in the *Journal of the American Medical Association,* July 27, 1984, found a greater risk of coronary heart disease among people who led sedentary lifestyles. As described in Chapter 3, people who have had heart attacks are usually placed on an exercise program by their physicians shortly after initial recovery in order to reduce the possibility of another attack. Exercise is also valuable for preventing and treating hypertension, diabetes, and osteoporosis.

A growing number of exercise books are being written specifically for older people, including those who are wheelchair-bound or bedridden. Two good books for the middle and later years are

Fitness After Forty: An Exercise Prescription for Lifelong Health by Herbert DeVries and Dianne Hales (Scribner's, 1982) and *Bonnie Prudden's After Fifty Fitness Guide* (Ballantine Books, 1987).

Exercising Your Trouble Spots. There are specific exercises that can greatly improve your appearance if undertaken on a regular basis.

A *protruding abdomen* can be controlled (together with dieting) by lying flat on your back on the floor, knees bent, hands under head and lifting your head and shoulders as far off the floor as you can, holding this position for a few counts. Keep your eyes focused on a spot over your head on the ceiling. Gradually work up to a count of ten. Do this up to ten or fifteen times a day. You will feel your stomach muscles tighten as you lift off the floor.

Improving *back muscles* will help your stomach muscles as well as prevent or alleviate back pain. As much as 80 percent of backaches are due to muscle fatigue rather than slipped discs or arthritis. Lie on your back, squeeze your buttocks together, and tighten stomach muscles while flattening your back against the floor. Hold for a count of five, then relax. Repeat ten times. Swimming is also excellent for those with back problems.

In later years many women develop *weakened pelvic muscles,* which makes them feel the vagina is losing its gripping ability. The Kegel exercises for women consist of twenty to thirty contractions of the muscles of the pelvic floor, as though one were holding oneself back from urinating and defecating at the same time. It should be possible to feel the muscles tightening. Perform these exercises several times daily while in either a sitting or standing position. Hold contractions for only a few seconds. The process must be repeated daily for at least one hundred contractions for the Kegel exercises to be truly effective.

When there is improved muscle tone as a result of using the Kegel exercises, the vaginal walls exert greater pressure on the penis. This is of particular value in those older couples where the man's penis has become somewhat smaller and the woman's vagina larger. Some women are able to use the Kegel movement in a rhythmic fashion during sexual intercourse, increasing the satisfaction of both partners. The exercises also help to support the pelvic structure—the uterus, bladder, and rectum. Some physicians prescribe Kegel exercises to treat or prevent prostatitis in men.

Nutrition

If you are over sixty, beware of poor nutrition and even malnutrition. You may protest, "But that's absurd! I've always eaten a normal diet." But poor nutrition can creep up on you in later life. Medical and lay people alike share the illusion that the United States is the world's best-fed nation. This is not true, and it is especially not true for older people. There are many reasons for this, the most obvious being the rising cost of good-quality food and the lowered incomes of many people, especially women, as they grow older. But there are other, less obvious reasons. Social isolation and depression can cause people to lose their appetites and stop taking an interest in cooking; physical limitations may make shopping and preparing food difficult; loss of teeth or poor teeth interfere with eating solid foods; illnesses, alcoholism, and chronic diseases of many kinds can affect food consumption; and, finally, poor eating habits may develop (snacking, the tea-and-toast syndrome, use of junk and convenience foods like TV dinners). Those who live alone are especially prone to neglect proper diets—"It's too much bother to fix a meal for just one person."

What are the dangers of poor nutrition? You become more vulnerable to disease. You fatigue more easily and lose a sense of well-being. You are more likely to have emotional problems, among them depression, apathy, anxiety. Age-related processes can be accelerated, and sexual interest and performance are often lowered. Thus you have a great many reasons to eat well, aside from the well-known pleasures of food itself.

A healthy diet includes three kinds of foods—proteins (meat, dairy products, eggs, fish, poultry, beans, nuts, and some grains), carbohydrates (cereals, breads, vegetables, fruits), and fats (meat, dairy products, oils, nuts, and grains).

Carbohydrates, the complex starches and natural sugars in fruits, vegetables, and grains, are emerging as the overall healthiest foods, supplemented by poultry, fish, and low-fat dairy products. Red meat, any kind of animal or dairy fat, and egg yolks should be strictly limited. Refined carbohydrates are often the most tempting foods, and both sweet tooths, who love sugar, and people who find starchy foods filling may overload their diets with them. Refined starches, sugar, and other sweeteners fill the stomach, raise the blood sugar, lower the appetite, and lead to a false sense of well-being. Do not be deceived. You must have some proteins every day for vitality and body-tissue repair. If cost is a problem, learn more about preparing foods "from scratch," using low-cost proteins (dried skim milk, dried beans, cheaper cuts of meat, etc.). The home economics departments of high schools or colleges near you can offer advice, as will the U.S. Department of Agriculture. Write to the Superintendent of Documents, Government Printing Office, Washington, DC 20402 for nutrition information. In general, cut down on desserts, pastries, fat meats, gravies, beer, sweet wines, hard liquors, and soft drinks. Natural sources of sugar, like frozen orange juice, are better for you and cheaper than many other products made from refined white sugar. Use vegetable oils and margarines that are low in saturated fats, and use less butter, lard, cream, and margarines high in saturated fats.

If you happen to be overweight and need to diet, a good general reference is *Jane Brody's Nutrition Book* (W. W. Norton, 1981), as well as *Jane Brody's Good Food Book* (W. W. Norton, 1985). Avoid crash and fad diets since they can harm your health and your appearance. Develop food habits you can live with comfortably in good health while still losing weight. Diet clubs such as TOPS, Weight Watchers, and Overeaters Anonymous, or self-organized weight clubs can make it easier for people with persistent weight problems to lose weight.

Diets aimed at prevention of disease are important far before age sixty. We know a good deal, for example, about diet and the prevention and control of heart disease. The earliest of the heart disease prevention diets is the Prudent Man's Diet, devised by Dr. Norman Jolliffe in 1957 and updated regularly. This is a balanced, low-calorie diet that lowers the amount of saturated fats and cholesterol you eat. It calls for a total of 2,400 calories a day (compared to the American male's average of 3,200), with no more than 30 percent fat, a cholesterol limit of 300 mg a day (roughly the amount in one egg), moderate protein, increased complex carbohydrates such as vegetables and fruits, and a reduction of salt. Low-fat recipes and cooking advice can be obtained from local heart associations or from the American Heart Association, 205 East 42nd Street, New York, NY 10017. *The Long Life Cookbook* by Anne Casale (Ballantine Books, 1988) is also a good source of recipes and information.

To help inform you more specifically about cholesterol, we list the following information from the National Institutes of Health Consensus Development Conference on Cholesterol (December 1984) and other recent studies:

▶ The average blood cholesterol for all Americans today is 210 mg. For older people, a cholesterol level of 240–260 mg (per deciliter of blood) indicates moderate risk of heart attack, while levels above 260 mg are at high risk.

▶ Cholesterol levels below 180 in men may increase the risk of colon cancer, so drastic reductions of cholesterol levels may not be wise.

▶ A specific sub-fraction of high-density-lipoprotein (HDL) cholesterol, called HDL_2, may protect against heart attack. Recent studies indicate that an extended program of regular aerobic exercise raises HDL_2.

▶ Fatty fish, such as salmon and mackerel, and monounsaturated fats, such as olive oil, may have cholesterol-lowering effects, according to recent research.

▶ Nearly all clinical trials of the effects of cholesterol lowering have focused on middle-aged men. We know much less about the elderly. Some feel that the very frail elderly should not restrict their cholesterol intake because of the risk of inadequate nutrients.

Other tips for older people:

▶ Go easy on salt since you are more susceptible to high blood pressure.

▶ Bulk in your diet is important for digestion. Doctors used to prescribe low-residue (limited-bulk) diets for older people with bowel problems, but now just the opposite is generally true. Bulk can be obtained by eating fruits and vegetables (complex carbohydrates) like raw celery, apples, and carrots, as well as wholegrain bread and cereals. This is true for all older people but especially for those who are dieting to lose weight. Bran cereal is good. If you want lots of bulk at low cost, buy coarse bran (local health-food stores usually carry it) for a few cents a pound. If you don't live near a health food store, get a mail-order healthfood catalog. Coarse bran tastes like a cross between babies' pabulum and sawdust, but if you take several teaspoonfuls in between swallows of fruit juice at each meal or a larger amount on your breakfast cereal daily, you will be taking an important step in promoting good bowel action and preventing diverticulosis, certain kinds of constipation, and other bowel problems. Bran is far better for you than laxatives. The complex carbohydrates may be even better.

▶ Try to avoid getting into the habit of taking laxatives, which can in fact induce habitual constipation. As we have noted, a good diet with plenty of bulk and plenty of exercise are the best ways to prevent constipation in later life. If you do need an occasional laxative, many doctors feel that milk of magnesia is preferable to mineral oil, which tends to reduce the absorption of fat-soluble vitamins.

▶ "Indigestion" from eating fried foods may mean gallstones; consult your doctor. Some liver specialists believe that a low-fat diet can help prevent formation of gallstones.

▶ Gout, arthritis, diabetes, and a number of other diseases that can directly affect your sex life as well as your general health may require a special diet prescribed by your doctor.

▶ Some people, more often women than men, have a bumpy kind of fat know as cellulite on their thighs and hips that resembles the texture of the skin of an orange. It can hang from upper arms or droop around the stomach. Dieting alone will not remove it. There are no reliable techniques for getting rid of this bothersome fat, but exercise and diet may help.

▶ If you tend to neglect your nutrition or are under stress, take a standard vitamin-and-mineral supplement. For the average healthy individual, a multivitamin should contain no more than 100 to 150 percent of the U.S. Recommended Daily Allowance (RDA) for any one nutrient.

▶ Anemia may occur when your diet is inadequate in iron and protein. Foods containing iron are lean meats, dark green leafy vegetables, and whole grain and enriched breads and cereals. The dietary approach is more economical and just as effective as the highly advertised vitamin-and-mineral preparations. (Remember that anemia should be evaluated by your doctor.)

▶ Osteoporosis, a common disorder, is due to a gradual loss of calcium from the bones, accelerated in women by the menopause. Wrist and hip fractures and deformities such as a hump on the back may develop. Factors that increase the risk of osteoporosis are high protein and salt intake, cigarette smoking, heavy caffeine and alcohol intake, lack of exercise, and a family history of osteoporosis. Osteoporosis may be slowed and possibly prevented in some women by nutrition and exercise, although specific recommendations are still under debate. For example, opinions differ on the significance of calcium intake, and some believe an excess of protein in the diet may be even more significant than insufficient calcium. For those greatly at risk (your doctor can help you evaluate your risk), estrogen replacement therapy currently is considered the most effective treatment, but because of its known risks, such treatment needs to be carefully evaluated by the patient and her doctor (see Chapter 2). Prevention of this disease should begin in middle age through adequate calcium intake—1,000 mg before menopause and 1,500 mg after it. The average intake of adult women is 450–500 mg a day—far too low. About five eight-ounce glasses of skim milk (to avoid fat intake) would supply 1,500 mg of calcium. If you don't like milk or it does not agree with you, calcium supplements containing carbonate, such as regular Tums, may be taken. Food containing calcium includes yogurt, hard cheese (especially Parmesan and Swiss), canned salmon and sardines (eat the bones too), kidney and pinto beans, bean curd, oysters, and collard, turnip, and mustard greens.

Postmenopausal women should not take more than the recommended amount of 1,500 mg of calcium because of possibly harmful effects from larger doses. Those with high blood pressure or a tendency to develop kidney stones, ulcers, or other digestive disorders may react adversely to high calcium intake.

▶ Large doses of vitamin E have been recommended for a variety of disorders, including sterility and vascular diseases, and for retarding the aging process, curing impotence, and healing wounds and burns. There is as yet no convincing scientific evidence for these claims. The recommended daily allowance for women is 20 to 25 international units (IU) and for men 30 IU.

▶ In general, be prudent about taking over-the-counter medications widely advertised on television and radio; they are sometimes valueless, often costly, and on occasion—especially if you take them in large quantities or combine them—hazardous. An office visit to your doctor may prove less expensive as well as better for your health than self-diagnosis and self-administered remedies for a physical complaint.

▶ It is a common belief that people need fewer calories as they grow older. One source claims that your body will require

10 percent fewer calories between ages thirty-five and fifty-five than when you were under thirty-five, 16 percent fewer between ages fifty-five and seventy-five, and 1 percent fewer calories per year for every year over seventy-five. We are not totally convinced. We suspect that this theory is based on the fact that many older people become less active and fail to work or exercise their bodies, and that caloric needs are a function of activity and not of age. Some inactivity is of course related to physical ailments, but much more is simply lack of motivation and inertia. The older you get, the more temptation you will feel to take it easy. Remember the maxim "Most people don't wear out, they rust out." Lack of movement leads to poor appetite, which in turn leads to fatigue and a vicious cycle.

▶ You will find that you feel and sleep better if you make your evening meal relatively light. (Breakfast is a good time to eat heartily.) Cutting down on food and alcohol intake before bed is also conducive to better sex. If you have had a heavy evening meal, it is best to postpone sex for a few hours to avoid unnecessary strain on the heart and other organs.

Rest

A rested body enhances sexual desire, improves sexual performance, and contributes to general health and well-being. Contrary to general opinion, as you grow older you will need as much sleep as when you were younger, or more. You may, however, notice changes in your sleep patterns. Studies show that older people seem to experience less "deep" or "delta" sleep (the period of dreamless oblivion) and become "lighter" sleepers, with more frequent awakenings. In addition, depression, anxiety, grief, loneliness, and lack of exercise can affect sleep patterns and depth of sleep. Early morning awakening is more common among the inactive, the depressed, those who go to bed early, and those who take frequent long naps during the day.

Get seven to ten hours of sleep a night, according to your needs. This varies from person to person. You need more sleep if you have physical health problems. Take one or more brief naps or rest breaks during the day and stretch out in bed.

If insomnia strikes, don't panic. To prepare for sleep, avoid caffeine drinks like coffee, tea, and colas before bedtime since they can keep you awake. Decaffeinated coffee is preferable, although some report that even the minimal amount of caffeine it contains can keep them awake. The establishment of simple rituals can get you psychologically ready for sleep: warm baths, firm and comfortable bed and pillows, back massage by a partner, reading a book, watching TV, or listening to music. Often warm milk, a glass of wine, a soothing talk with your partner, or a phone call to an understanding friend can comfort you and relax your tensions. Exercise can have a positive effect on sleep if completed early enough in the day, particularly if it has been performed regularly for at least two months. But exercise should be avoided for two hours before bedtime to avoid insomnia brought about by stimulation of the body.

Bedtime is a time when your defenses against anxiety, anger, and other emotions are down. If these create persistent troubled sleep or insomnia, psychotherapy or some form of counseling may help. Avoid nonprescription sleep remedies; they are expensive and largely useless. Eventually your body will become tired enough to sleep by itself. We don't recommend sleeping pills (hypnotics) unless you are in pain or great physical or emotional discomfort, because they can be habit-forming and may cause adverse side effects, including, paradoxically, the perpetuation of insomnia. The use of hypnotics should be evaluated by a physician on an ongoing basis—prescriptions should not be automatically renewed. Active, pleasurable sexual activity, including sexual self-stimulation, can be an excellent sleep inducer. This effect is strongest when there is orgasm, but even without it such activity is usually mildly relaxing.

For help with serious sleep disturbances and disorders, contact your physician. You may be able to find specialists in sleep disorders in your area by contacting the Association of Sleep

Disorders Centers, 604 2nd Street, S.W., Rochester, MN 55902. For example, the Geriatric Medicine Associates, Department of Geriatrics, at the Mount Sinai Medical Center in New York, have a program focused on sleep problems in middle and later life.

Hearing Problems

One out of every four older people has a hearing impairment. For a number of reasons—among them embarrassment, pride, a psychological determination to deny the fact—a surprising number of people refuse to use hearing aids even when aids will help. Not all hearing impairments can be improved by wearing a hearing aid, but only an audiologist (a specialist trained in a program accredited by the American Speech and Hearing Association) or an otologist or otolaryngologist (doctors specifically trained to treat ear disorders) can determine this; and if you suspect you have some hearing loss, you should consult with one of these specialists. Remember, too, that hearing impairments tend to develop gradually, so you may be unaware this is happening to you. If you find yourself frequently missing parts of ordinary conversation around you or have trouble making out the dialogue when you go to the movies, it is a good idea to have your hearing checked.

Impaired hearing isolates one from society far more than most people realize. Present-day hearing aids are much less conspicuous, disfiguring, and cumbersome than they used to be, and observers are likely to be very matter-of-fact about them. If yours is the type of loss that can be compensated for by the use of a hearing aid, do not let personal inhibitions stop you from using one. You will realize how much you have been missing only after your hearing improves.

It will take time for you to accustom yourself to a hearing aid, so be prepared for an adjustment period and stick with it despite discomfort at the start. You will probably find it helpful to notice how other people use their aids while you are learning to use yours. Thereafter, always use your aid whenever you are with another person.

Be very careful to deal only with a responsible supplier. This is a field full of high-pressure door-to-door salesmen offering "low" prices, "easy" installment payments, and defective or shoddy equipment. It is important that you be properly tested and fitted with an aid of good quality, appropriate to your needs.

People who have the kind of hearing loss that cannot be helped by a hearing aid must be frank with friends and intimates. It is unlikely that they will find this information embarrassing; the awkwardness is more likely to be on your side. Sit close to your companion so you can hear what is being said and speak up when you do not. It is only when you attempt to conceal a hearing impairment that problems are likely to arise.

Skin Care for Men and Women

Ideally, prevention of skin problems should begin in the early years for both men and women, but good skin care can help at any time in life. Skin can be damaged by too much sun or wind and by malnutrition, excess alcohol, disease, depression, drugs, and anxiety. Overexposure to the sun causes more premature aging, particularly in Caucasians, than any other factor. Sunbathing and working or playing out of doors unprotected for long periods of time are the major culprits. They can result in permanent skin damage affecting both the outer and inner layers of skin, causing loss of water and elasticity, deep wrinkles, and grooves. Prolonged exposure to very cold weather, overheated rooms with minimal humidity, and air conditioning in warm climates can deplete the moisture in the skin, making it look lined. Electric blankets left on all night can dry the body skin. Various kinds of air pollution can be damaging. Poor nutrition, whether vitamin deficiencies or unbalanced diets, can cause dry, scaly, and inelastic skin. Sagging skin sometimes follows too rapid weight loss. Anxiety, depression, and tension speed up the appearance of aging. Cigarette smoking can cause wrinkles to appear sooner than they normally would, since nicotine narrows the small capillaries and cuts down the supply of blood bringing nourishment and oxygen to the skin.

Even with the best of preventive care, the human face begins to acquire noticeable lines and wrinkles around the age of forty. There is a gradual permanent loss of elasticity in both the skin and the underlying tissue. Wrinkles per se should not become an obsessive concern; looking your age does not mean looking unattractive. The facial changes of aging are aspects of individuality. But all of us—even those not enmeshed in the cult of youth—want to look our best. Don't waste your money on "wrinkle removers" and other gimmicks "guaranteed" to make you look younger. Anything that keeps the skin moist will help to slow down the appearance of aging.

Here is a simple regimen that can be followed by those women and men who want to take care of their skin. Thorough cleansing of the face and neck is important as the first step. Many older people can tolerate a mild soap like Camay if it is used quickly and rinsed off completely. Neutrogena, which is much more expensive, is also a possibility, or a rinsable cleanser, which combines cream and a small amount of soap in lotion form. (Creams and oils used alone are difficult to remove, so the skin is never completely cleansed.) After cleansing and a thorough rinsing with warm water, pat the face dry and immediately protect it with a light moisturizer by day or a heavier oily cream for night while the skin still holds the moisture absorbed from the rinse. Most inexpensive dime-store creams work as well as expensive ones. (Cosmetics and creams can be purchased at a reduced price through the pharmacy service provided for members of the American Association of Retired Persons. For information write NRTA-AARP Pharmacy, 1909 K Street, N.W., Washington, DC 20006.) About once a week, women should rub something rough on the face such as cleansing grains or inexpensive corn meal on a wet washcloth. This helps remove the outer layer of dry flaky cells. (Men need not do this since shaving accomplishes the same purpose.) The body itself can also be protected against drying by using a body lotion immediately after a bath or shower when the skin has absorbed moisture.

Electric facial saunas dry the skin. The face should really not be massaged, but if you must do it, never stretch or pull the skin in any downward direction. Various chemical processes and dermabrasion (removal of the tissues of the outer skin layer with a rotating wire brush) can be dangerous unless done by skilled operators. They are also expensive. Plastic surgery (face lifts) for both men and women can correct severe skin sagging, but they, too, are expensive, and good results last only three to five years. The best skin care is sensible cleansing, good diet, rest and lack of tension, and avoidance of too much sun, wind, cigarette smoking, and alcohol.

Chapter 6

Common Emotional Problems
With Sex

S exual problems in the later years may be caused by upsetting events in your life, such as the death of a loved one, retirement, relationship conflicts, or simply too much stress and worry. Growing older itself can be frightening, especially if you don't know what to expect or how to handle it. Your early life experience and your society's attitudes have their impact as well.

Personal Anxieties

A major emotional problem for the older man is the *fear* of sexual impotence. Some men have to deal with actual impotence, which is usually temporary. *Impotence occurs occasionally in nearly all men of all ages* for a variety of reasons—among them fatigue, tension, illnesses, and excessive drinking. In most cases potency returns by itself without specific treatment when the causative physical or emotional condition is reversed. In later life, however, certain men do begin to have chronic difficulty in obtaining and maintaining an erection. Some find that their capacity for sexual intercourse is greatly diminished or disappears completely. We discussed the possible organic causes of impotence in Chapter 3. But many problems are psychologically caused. The sex organs are a barometer of a man's feelings and quickly reflect his state of mind and current life situation. The nerve connections that control the penis are extremely sensitive to emotions. Anxiety, fear, and anger are the primary feelings that can cause a man to lose an erection rapidly or fail to achieve one in the first place. A disturbance in sexual functioning is often one of the first indications of unusual stress or emotional problems.

Men who do not know about the *normal* physiological changes in their sexual behavior that come with aging may believe falsely that they are becoming impotent. The expectation of high performance, which is taught to males from childhood on through constant emphasis on competition and winning, leads many men to overemphasize the physical-performance aspect of their sexuality. They become focused on erections and ejaculations rather than on expressing their feelings. This makes impotence or even its threat greatly upsetting. The *fear* of impotence can *cause* impotence. The harder a man tries to have an erection, the less likely he is to succeed. Impotence does not respond to will power and force. If it is truly transitory, it is much more likely to improve with relaxation and freedom from pressure.

Unresponsive sexual partners can threaten men and lead to impotence. A woman's disinterest or perfunctory acquiescence is very likely to affect her partner. Women may also become impatient or demanding and make a transitory potency problem more severe. Some find impotence threatening to their own self-esteem and react with hostility or hurt. They see it as a sign of disinterest in them or a failure on their part to be sexually attractive.

Emotional and physical fatigue, boredom with routine lovemaking, overwork, and worries about family or finances can all affect potency. Impotence is often one of the first symptoms of depression. Disappointment, sadness, and grief over personal losses can be factors. So can resentfulness and irritation.

Sometimes impotence is a result of hidden fear of death or injury. Fred Patterson, a businessman and retired Army officer, had been a vigorous and sexually active man until he suffered a coronary attack. After the attack he was unable to have an erec-

99

tion. It took many sessions with a psychiatrist to help him recognize that his fear that sexual activity might bring on another coronary was the reason he did not allow himself to have an erection. His doctors agreed to a provisional program of exercise, including sex, which would not jeopardize his heart. As Patterson's anxiety lessened through psychotherapeutic counseling, and his sense of well-being increased as a result of his physical fitness program, his sexual ability returned.

A sudden attack of impotence is likely to be the result of some unusual stress and will usually abate when the stress is relieved. If impotence continues for any considerable period of time, information and reassurance from a doctor or professional counselor may be all that is needed. If the impotence still persists, however, comprehensive medical evaluation and more extended psychotherapy and/or sexual counseling may be required. The cooperation and support of one's partner are important in overcoming impotence.

Women are somewhat less subject to fear of sexual dysfunctioning in later life than men, largely because they do not have to worry about erection. Except for possible menopausal changes, the normal physical changes that accompany aging interfere little with female sexual ability. Unlike most men, women can perform the sex act even when they are emotionally upset or uninterested. They may not enjoy lovemaking or have an orgasm in such situations, but they are physically capable of having intercourse. (They may, however, worry about orgasmic capacity, much as men are concerned about erection and ejaculatory capacity.) Indeed, in later life some women become more relaxed about sex and may even come to enjoy it more when the menopause has freed them from fears of unwanted pregnancies. Their responsibilities diminish when their children leave home, and the "empty nest" is frequently a welcome event rather than a problem.

But women can have other problems. Many older men and women grew up believing that "nice" women were not interested in sex and indeed found it distasteful. They were traditionally admonished or conditioned to be passive, resigned, and accepting; it was "loose" women who gave themselves to the pleasures of sex or sought it. A nineteenth-century marriage manual advised: "As a general rule, a modest woman seldom desires any sexual gratification for herself. She submits to her husband, but only to please him; and, but for the desire of maternity, would far rather be relieved from his attentions." Women may remember being taught that sex was simply a duty. Men were the pursuers, women reluctant and pursued. Such ingrained attitudes interfere with the development of close relationships in which partners share openly in the enjoyment of sex. If this has been your experience, frank talks with your partner can help clear up antiquated assumptions.

The most profound emotional and sexual difficulties for older women revolve around the possibility of finding themselves alone —widowed, divorced, separated, or single—as they grow older. Their lives are affected by one major fact: there are not enough men to go around. In the United States in 1985 there were 11.5 million men aged sixty-five or over and 17 million women. This disparity increases year by year as time passes, for two reasons. First, women outlive men by an average of seven years. (In 1985 life expectancy from birth was 78.2 years for females and 71.2 years for males, according to the Census Bureau.) Second, women marry men an average of three years older than themselves. Of the 17 million women over sixty-five, over 8 million were widowed and 1.5 million were divorced or single.

The "Old Person" Trap

Even when their physical and mental health is excellent, men and women in their fifties, sixties, and seventies sometimes exhibit an old-man or old-woman act as though they were tottering invalids on their last legs. Having a rigid, stereotyped, desexualized image of what an older person *should* be, they play the role with stubborn determination. The "old-person act" allows them to avoid responsibility toward themselves and others and to evoke sympathy. It is a symptom of demoralization and giving up.

Certain older people decide that sexual ability is gone and arbitrarily declare themselves sexually incapacitated. Angry or obstinate refusal to discuss the issue with the partner or to consider possible remedies is typical in these instances. Behind this stance is an effort to avoid anxiety about sex or a sexual relationship.

Some older people decide they are ugly and undesirable and begin to hate the way they look. They make frantic attempts to appear young but may become depressed over the hopelessness of altering their appearance significantly. Another variation of self-hatred is found in those people who look into the mirror and insist that what they see "is not the real me." They may decide that their only true self is interior and refuse to accept or identify with their physical characteristics. Although it may take some time, it is essential to accept the realities of change as part of one's self.

Sometimes the angry response of older people to their own sexual and social deprivation is hostility toward those who are younger. Everyone has heard bitter threats such as "You'll see what it's like when *you're* old" or "Wait until you reach *my* age— you won't be so smart." There may also be self-righteous criticism of the sexuality of their own contemporaries as well as of the young.

Older men and women can make a self-fulfilling prophecy of sexual failure. Overwhelmed and demoralized by the unattractive picture drawn by society of late life, they literally give up without trying, or guarantee their own failure when they do try. To anticipate failure is to cause it to happen. If you think yourself unattractive, you tend to become so. If you believe you are sexually ineligible, you are likely to hide yourself away from opportunities that might lead to social and sexual encounters.

Sexual Guilt and Shame

Sexual guilt and shame are factors in many people's reaction to sex. These feelings derive from childhood and family experiences, and from the sexual searchings of childhood, which are so often confusing and disturbing. People past sixty, often brought up in a period of Victorian-like prudery, are likely to have been treated to more than their share of misinformation, made to feel guilty about any sexual stirrings they sensed, and given few chances to get satisfying answers to their questions—if they dared ask them. The culture insisted that childhood was innocent of sexuality, and any normal expression of it, verbal or physical —looking, feeling, talking, touching—was often punished.

Masturbation was strictly forbidden. The Victorians invented a grotesque array of mechanical devices to make certain that children, particularly boys, would not be able to stimulate themselves. Children were warned that masturbation could cause feeblemindedness or madness; it could "use up the life juices," weaken the body and shorten the life span, and make one nervous, distracted, and highstrung. Dark circles under the eyes were alleged indications of secret masturbation, and a grisly folklore sprang up in which hands withered and fell off if they were used in sexual stimulation.

An important misassumption that many older men still have from their youth is that "too much" sexual activity reduces potency and lowers semen "reserves." The belief that semen must be conserved is sheer nonsense because it is constantly produced—yet in 1937 a sex hygiene manual from the U.S. Public Health Service was still warning youths not to "waste vital fluids," and the 1945 edition of the *Boy Scout Manual* repeated these words.

Because for older men and women the greater part of their procreative years occurred before birth control techniques were as sophisticated, reliable, and freely available as they are today, spontaneous sexual enjoyment was often hampered by the fear of pregnancy. Chronic and justified fears of venereal disease, for which effective drugs had not yet been devised, also laid psychological inhibitions on sexuality. So did many traditional religious teachings.

The habit-forming effects of such long-term constraints tend to linger, and it is often hard for older people to give themselves freely to sexual expression. It is not easy to overcome ingrained guilt and shame even when your better judgment tells you that sexuality need no longer be considered evil or dangerous. Thinking through your own childhood and early adult experiences may help you understand your present feelings better. Remember once again that sexual problems, whether caused by personal or by social factors, are rarely insurmountable.

Problems Between Partners

Problems in the relationship with one's sexual partner can very quickly affect sexual functioning. An angry, bored, or otherwise unresponsive sexual partner can lead to potency problems for men and sexual disinterest or lack of response for women.

Low sexual interest rather than impotence per se may be a central problem for many men. Dr. Joseph Lo Piccolo of Texas A & M University believes that chronic low sex drive is much more common among men than was previously thought. He describes most of this as psychologically based, ranging from the effects of feeling overwhelmed by life events to fears of intimacy.

Women, according to Dr. Lo Piccolo, are becoming more likely to question male performance and behavior and are often the ones who initiate treatment for the male with low sexual interest. But women themselves may exhibit the symptoms. Called "frigidity," this behavior used to be interpreted as fear and active resistance to sexuality, but now it is more often viewed as low sexual desire and lack of responsiveness.

Although a lack of sexual desire can be a comfortable way of life for some, it is more often troubling to at least one partner. Sex therapists note that a growing proportion of their patients seek help for what is currently called "inhibited sexual desire." Drs. Raul Schiavi and Patricia Schreiner-Engel of Mount Sinai Hospital's Human Sexuality Program in New York City are studying low sexual desire in a growing effort to understand the phenomenon.

Occasional and short-lived lack of sexual desire is commonplace and reversible. But if low sexual desire is long-lasting, it can be one of the most difficult and intractable of sexual symptoms. For those who wish to change, a combination of sex therapy, psychotherapy, and marriage counseling over an extended period of time may prove beneficial.

When sexual desire is present but physical responsiveness is absent, manifested as impotence in men and failure to lubricate and reach orgasm in women, the causes can be a range of emotions from depression, grief, and stress to anxiety, fear, and anger. Sexual response ordinarily returns when the underlying emotions are resolved or improvement occurs. But such psychologically based symptoms, whatever their original emotional cause, can also quickly create performance anxiety and continued sexual problems if people are intimidated, embarrassed, or frightened by changes in their sexual functioning. This is particularly true of men for whom "performance" carries great importance.

The first step in self-treatment is for partners to relax and assume that sexual functioning is likely to improve once the emotional equilibrium is restored. Kindness and consideration toward each other and a lack of psychological pressure are crucial in providing space and time in which to recover. It is important to remember that sexual response cannot be willed. It is most likely to occur when a person is rested, relaxed, in a positive mood, and in good relation with his or her partner.

Physical stimulation, at first involving the body as a whole and later focusing on the genitals, is an important part of arousal. Masters and Johnson initiated a three-stage method of "sensate focus," which is now used by many sex therapists to teach people to relax and slowly move each other into a state of sexual arousal, eventually resulting in sexual climax. The stages are, first, a stepwise nongenital "pleasuring" of one's partner's body by touching and caressing; second, genital touching and caressing without intercourse; and third, nondemanding sexual intercourse where the goal is pleasure rather than performance.

Special techniques are also available to stop or slow premature ejaculation. Occasional and temporary premature ejaculation happens to most men from time to time, when they have had infrequent sex or are unusually aroused. It usually disappears by itself as circumstances change. Persistent premature ejaculation is another matter. It does not tend to develop for the first time in the mid or later years but usually evolves early on, and it may continue into later life. Fortunately it is subject to treatment. Reassurance is the first step to try, along with making certain there are regular opportunities for sexual outlet. If these efforts are not enough, a highly successful method has been developed —the "squeeze" technique—in which the woman grasps the end of her partner's erect penis where the shaft meets the glans and squeezes strongly with the thumb and first two fingers for several seconds. This causes the man to lose his urge to ejaculate but allows the couple to continue lovemaking. By alternating the squeezing with sex play, a couple may delay ejaculation until they are ready for a climax. The "stop-start" technique, perhaps the most frequent approach used, refers to stopping genital stimulation until the urge to ejaculate disappears—at which time stimulation is resumed again. If these techniques fail to work, psychotherapy can be helpful. In addition, premature ejaculation may become less of a problem as a man grows older, simply because some of the urgency to ejaculate diminishes.

Changes Over Time

Role changes over time can also cause disruptions. One or the other partner may alter his or her level of assertiveness, affecting the original emotional or power balance between the two. We sometimes see older relationships in which the man has assumed a predominantly fatherly, protective role toward his more dependent partner. He may call her "my baby" or "little girl" even in later life. If he becomes ill and requires her care, serious problems, including sexual difficulties, can arise. The woman, who has always been babied, can become petulant, dissatisified, or simply unable or unwilling to play a giving and responsible role. A variant of this is the hypochondriacal man—the worrywart—involved with an independent and caretaking woman who becomes ill. When she cannot mother her partner, the equilibrium in which they had functioned for so long is upset.

Most typically, women gradually become more assertive and men more nurturant as they grow older. This pattern appears to occur in numerous cultures studied. One of the explanations is that it represents a move toward "wholeness" of personality after the cultural and possibly biological emphasis on gender differences in behavior earlier in life, with young men assuming the assertive roles and young women the nurturing ones.

People may also simply grow tired of their usual roles and desperately desire a change. Sexual boredom and apathy are very common among older couples, who may fall into routine patterns in which they do the same things time after time, year after year, with little imagination in technique or style and a scarcity of zest for creating sexual excitement. The partners eventually may no longer even care for each other. A new partner may seem to bring improvement, but unless the sources of underlying boredom are dealt with, the improvement may prove only temporary after the novelty has worn off.

Interestingly, relationships that were unstable and unsatisfactory earlier in life sometimes improve in the later years, as the children grow up and leave and the stresses of parenthood and career pass. On the other hand, long-standing problems between partners can worsen as the result of chronic irritation from years of unresolved conflict. Personality and behavior changes may also be unilateral, as one partner begins to move in new directions, leaving the other behind, often angry and hurt.

What should you do if you and your partner are having problems? First, talk to each other about the problems—often. It is important to determine the basis of the problem and then to cooperate with each other in attempting to resolve it. Be prepared for the fact that each of you may refuse to admit your own contribution to the situation and may project the blame onto the other. It is difficult to be open and objective about emotional issues. But it is absolutely imperative to realize that what you should be looking for is a solution rather than a culprit. If you find you need help, go together to your clergyman, physician, or a professional psychotherapist or counselor. If your partner won't go, go alone. Late-life separation and/or divorce can be an extremely painful and jolting experience, and efforts should be made to salvage and improve difficult relationships first. Even if separation occurs, you will have learned something about yourself and your partner that may help you understand the past as you prepare for the future.

Life Cycle Changes

Divorce

Currently 50 percent of first marriages end in divorce. Of the divorced, 75 percent remarry, most within five years, and 60 percent divorce again. Of these, 75 percent marry for the third time. A flattening of the divorce rate in the past five years indicates that we may have stabilized at the current rates of divorce for the present. Some believe that the practical and psychological problems resulting from divorce and serial marriage will become so severe that there will be a trend back to preservation of first or at least second marriages through more skilled premarital and marital counseling (counseling now prevents divorce in only 10–15 percent of cases, and conciliations have even less success) and less accessible divorce. Others see the tendency toward "serial" marriages as natural and inevitable as people live longer, divorce is easier to obtain, and women are more independent financially.

The process of separation and divorce precipitates more couples into professional counseling than any other life crisis, simply because it is so common and so frequently painful. Current studies show that, at younger ages, men tend to have greater psychological adjustment problems after divorce than women, although women have far more economic problems, especially when there are minor children. In the older age groups, women appear to have the greater adjustment problems: their financial situation is more precarious, many have no work history outside the home, there are fewer men available for companionship and possible remarriage, and socially, older women alone are often seen as not fitting in or, even worse, stereotyped as boring and uninteresting.

The process of separation and divorce can have serious effects on one's belief in oneself as a socially and sexually desirable person, particularly if one's partner initiated the process. The challenge is to build relationships in which the divorced person feels support, social approval, friendship, and possibly a new intimacy with another person. We have outlined some suggestions for doing so later in Chapter 7.

Retirement

Retirement can bring problems as well as possibilities for enhancing relationships. The sudden onset of twenty-four hours a day of togetherness can be a difficult adjustment to make. Such unremitting intimacy places greater pressure on emotional relationships and brings problems into more acute focus. What may previously have been an occasional irritant can become constant. A struggle for power or simply control over daily activities can become a preoccupation as each partner strives to adjust to the frequent presence of the other. Even if you can work out these struggles, constant togetherness may dismay or disconcert or irritate you. It is essential that you find a balance between shared time and time alone to give each of you elbow room, and that you talk to your partner about your concerns.

Yet retirement has many advantages for couples. They have more time to devote to relationships, and many couples in fact become closer to each other and to other people after retirement. Schedules are also much more flexible, and one or both members of a couple are less likely to find themselves exhausted when the opportunity for intimacy arises.

Chronic and Incapacitating Illness

Illness may incapacitate one sexual partner physically and/or mentally but not the other, particularly when there is a substantial age gap between them. Frequently the man develops a serious illness first, leaving the woman without a companion or a sexual partner. Healthy women—especially those who are significantly younger than their husbands—may spend years in a relationship without adult intimacy or sexual contact. Other feelings can complicate the picture. When one partner becomes ill, the other ordinarily reacts with concern and the desire to help. But if the illness becomes chronic, the well partner may be surprised to find himself or herself filled with anger. This may reflect threat of the possible loss of the other; it can also represent overwork and exhaustion or an understandable resentment over missing out on life because of the duties of the nursing role and the incapacities of one's partner. It is important not to feel guilty about such resentments. Face them frankly and secure outside help whenever possible from your relatives, neighbors, friends, or professional homemakers to reduce the burden. Support groups involving people in similar circumstances can be very helpful. It may be necessary to begin to build new friendships to provide a sense of self-worth and companionship.

At other times illness may cause sexual problems, but both partners may still desire and be able to have a relationship that involves closeness and a sense of being valued. Intercourse is the form of sexual activity that is most likely to be impaired. Both partners may feel guilty and need to reassure each other that they can develop other satisfying methods to express sexuality. In general, the less goal-oriented (in terms of erections and orgasms) and the more flexible people are, the more likely they are to find ways to enjoy sex and each other.

Partners with ill or disabled mates at home state that it is difficult to routinely bathe, feed, and provide nursing care for a mate and still think of him or her as a sexually desirable person. If sexuality is otherwise viable and important to the couple, a visiting nurse or a home-help attendant, if affordable, should take care of the least aesthetic parts of patient care. A quick return to roles as normal as possible is the ideal. The expression of your feelings to someone you trust or possibly to your partner, accurate information about the physical problems of your partner, involvement in whatever rehabilitation process is feasible, and finding new ways to express caring and sexuality when necessary are all ways to adapt positively.

Knowledge that an illness of one partner may be terminal or fatal sometimes brings an improvement or a heightening of a relationship. Couples report that the certainty or closeness of death causes them to cherish the present moment and to take advantage of the time they have left together. When sexuality is a part of that closeness, such couples should always have the opportunity for privacy and time alone, even if one partner is confined to a hospital or another institution. If they encounter problems in working this out with the institution, a patient representative department or a social work staff may be available to help.

Institutional Living

The 5 percent of persons over sixty-five who live in homes for the aging, nursing homes, chronic-disease hospitals, and other long-term-care institutions are in general denied the opportunity for any private social and sexual life. Visitors are in full view of roommates and staff and can be overheard by them. Even those who have marital partners are seldom able to share conjugal visits, where the patient is afforded a private time and place with his or her partner.

Intimacies of any kind between unmarried fellow patients, even hugging or kissing or holding hands, are frowned on despite the fact that they are performed by consenting adults. Even persons who, understandably, resort to self-stimulation because they have no other sexual outlet run the risk of being discovered and reprimanded like children.

Most older persons in these situations are reluctant to complain to the management, even though their rights as adults are being seriously infringed on. Ask the administrator of your particular institution to provide whatever privacy you and other patients should have. If you need outside support, ask your relatives, friends, doctor, lawyer, or a member of the clergy to help you in stating your cause. Speak to patients who have a similar complaint and make it a joint project. You can also alert groups that are interested in the problems of older persons, such as local chapters of the Gray Panthers, the Older Women's League, the American Association of Retired Persons, and the National Council of Senior Citizens. Federal regulations issued on June 1, 1978, provide some right to privacy, but only for married couples, and only in nursing homes that participate in federal Medicare and Medicaid programs (more than two-thirds do not). These regulations are not being uniformly enforced but failure to observe them is ground for legal action. For information, write Health Standards and Quality Bureau, Office of Standards and Certification, Health Care Financing Administration, Rockville, MD 20857.

Widowhood

The possibility of widowhood increases with age. The losses and grieving that are inevitable as we grow older need to be worked through and accepted in order that the survivor be freed psychologically to resume a full life or shape a new and different one. Losing someone you have loved—partner, friend, child— usually means shock and then a long, slow journey through grief. Acute grief, with intense mental anguish and remorse, ordinarily lasts a month or two and then begins to lessen. In most cases, grief works itself out in six to eighteen months, unless it is complicated by further loss, stress, or other factors. *Widow shock*, an exaggerated state that can follow the sudden and un-

expected death of a partner, or occurs when the surviving partner is ill-prepared to handle living alone, leaves the survivor
unable to accept death and take up life again. To recover, he or
she needs to be encouraged to grieve and should be given assistance in building an active life once more. The open expression
of feelings, including crying, is important for both men and
women in resolving grief. Sharing one's sadness, anger, resentment, fear, and self-pity with someone helps.

Such *grief work* also involves talking about your sexual feelings. People need to separate out their own identities from the
commingling of identities that has occurred in close and long-
term relationships. The feeling that "part of me died with him
[her]" can then be replaced with the feeling that "I am a person
in myself and I am still alive." A man may find himself temporarily
impotent, a symptom we call widower's syndrome, which usually
clears up if he is encouraged to grieve and find his way through
the loss.

Anticipatory grief, during which a person undergoes an extended grief reaction period to the expected death of the loved
one—as happens in the course of a terminal illness—can soften
the shock of death. Such grieving may result in a closer relationship with the ill partner, but there are instances when the grieving person may close himself or herself off, as though the partner
were already dead. When this occurs, outside counseling help
may be needed to reestablish the relationship with the dying
person.

After the death of a partner, it is often very difficult for the
man or woman who has been widowed to look ahead to a new
partner without feelings of guilt or disloyalty to the memory of
the dead one. In *enshrinement,* the survivor keeps things just as
they were when the loved one was alive and spends his or her
energy revering the memory of the dead person, surrounded by
photographs and rooms maintained intact. The survivor believes
that to live fully is a betrayal of love or loyalty for the dead. This
survival guilt and fear of infidelity leads to emotional stagnation

and stands in the way of achieving new relationships. Once the period of mourning is over and the initial shock and grief have abated, you owe it to yourself to become realistic about your need to have a new life of your own. This means the appropriate preservation of your memories without excessive dwelling in the past. The usual cure for enshrinement is to take an active role in getting life moving again. This is an act of will and determination. It can happen only if the individual decides to make it happen. Removing from sight the personal possessions of the deceased will help. It may also be necessary to put away obvious marriage symbols, such as the wedding ring. It is not a betrayal of a past marriage to accept the present and build a future.

If grief and anger over a death continue unchanged for years, something is interfering with the natural healing process of time. Quite often it is unresolved negative feelings toward the dead person, as in an unhappy marriage, or a stubborn refusal to accept fate (an adult temper tantrum) and to take positive steps toward creating a new life. In these cases, professional counseling help may be necessary.

For those age fifty-five or older, the American Association of Retired Persons (AARP) has a Widowed Persons Service in 170 locations nationwide. A volunteer who has gone through the same experience will be sent to talk to the newly widowed person about his or her feelings, and help with problems. Also available is a *Survival Handbook for Widows*.

Homosexual Relationships

Many people, including many homosexuals themselves, particularly men, believe that life becomes increasingly bleak and lonely as the homosexual person grows older. This is by no means inevitably true. Between 5 and 10 percent or more of all Americans are homosexual; many have long-term relationships, are emotionally stable, and see themselves as successful and happy.

When difficulties, both social and sexual, occur for homosexual couples, they involve many of the same interpersonal problems faced by heterosexual couples. In addition, however, homosexual couples may find themselves isolated in the larger society, with few role models for growing older in a homosexual relationship or as single people. There can be lack of support when a partner of long standing is ill or dies. Hospitals and other institutions may not recognize the homosexual relationship in terms of visitation privileges and consultation with medical personnel. Legal rights are often unclear and unprotected; for example, wills can be contested by relatives if belongings are left to a homosexual partner.

Organizations are beginning to form to aid homosexuals as they reach the mid and later years. An organization called SAGE (Senior Action in a Gay Environment) in New York City offers a variety of social services to older members and promotes the opportunity for intergenerational support. The National Association of Lesbian and Gay Gerontologists is actively promoting understanding and services for the homosexual community in mid and later life. (For information, write NALGG, 3312 Descosso Drive, Los Angeles, CA 90026.) *Legal Guide for Lesbian and Gay Couples* by Denis Clifford and Hayden Curry (Nolo Press, 1986) is one of the books that cover the financial aspects of homosexual relationships. Specific sexual issues for male homosexuals are currently dominated by the AIDS epidemic, as described in Chapter 3.

Chapter 7

People Without Partners: Finding New Relationships

The Demographic Dilemma

As they grow older, many people find themselves without partners. This is especially true of women because of their longer life expectancies and lower rates of remarriage after widowhood. Until medical science and public health techniques become more successful in equalizing the life expectancy of men and women, we shall have to tolerate the social consequences of greater numbers of partnerless women over sixty than partnerless men. However, women are adapting in a number of ways: by challenging negative cultural stereotypes of them, both personally and institutionally through organizations like the Older Women's League and the Gray Panthers; by learning to take the initiative in building friendships and a social life; and by redefining their own sexuality to include a wider range of options for satisfying intimacy and sexual release. Some are developing relationships with younger men. Others have relationships with married men who may be unable or unwilling to leave their marriages. Some sublimate their sexuality by developing absorbing activities that bring them companionship and accomplishment. Homosexual women are in a particularly advantageous spot as they reach midlife and beyond, since partners who are their own age will have the same life expectancy and they move in a world that becomes increasingly female with each decade.

None of this, however, is a wholly satisfying substitute for increasing the life expectancy of men as well as preserving their physical vigor and sexual functioning as they grow older. Fortunately, we are already seeing improvements, with a dramatic drop in deaths from heart disease since the early 1970s for both black and white males and more recently, a drop in lung cancer death rates for white males.

The likelihood of losing your partner is a fact of late life that increases with time. In 1985, more than half of all women over sixty were widowed, as compared to about 14 percent of men. Another 5 percent of men and women this age had never married, and about 4 percent were divorced. Obviously there are differences between the life-style of those who never married and who over the years have created a circle of friends and intimates that substitutes for an immediate family, and those who are abruptly separated from a spouse by death or divorce and now find themselves on their own for the first time in many years or possibly in their lives. Where the widowed person is deprived of the shared intimacies and interdependence of long marriage and the social patterns that go with being a couple, the single or long-divorced man or woman is accustomed to living on his or her own. Still, as one grows older, time and deaths erode the circle of relatives and close friends regardless of marital status, and some people find an increasing emptiness in the later years that needs to be filled.

Building a New Social Life

You cannot depend on the healing power of time alone to ease grief or loss or to alleviate loneliness. New relationships will not simply happen. You will have to take an active part in putting your life together again.

Where Do You Start?

Initiative is the first requisite. It is up to you to take charge of your life, to decide what you want and what you should do about it. This does not mean you must deliberately be searching for a possible partner. You may want no more than opportunities to meet people who are congenial and likely to share your own interests. One way to do this is to look for activities that support these interests. You will feel less tense and pressured if you are doing what you like to do. A sense of pleasure and purpose in what you are doing will encourage you to enjoy, learn, give of yourself, and make friends.

Some People Worry About Etiquette

Many older people are still bound by the customs they were taught as youngsters, and many of these formalities make no sense today. Women used to be told it was improper to call a man. But if you are interested, you do not have to wait for invitations from a man; simply behave as you do when you want to get in touch with a friend. He has the option of accepting or refusing just as you do when a man (or woman) calls you. If he accepts your invitation, a friendship or a relationship may develop or it may not—but you will have taken a perfectly appropriate and dignified initiative that allows you an *active* role in finding new friends and activities.

What Activities Should You Try?

A variety of activities are available to older people without partners who want to develop a fuller social life. Among the best opportunities are those afforded through work. If you do not have a job but are interested and able, consider the possibility of looking actively for part-time work, both for the rewards of being useful and for the opportunities it offers to meet new people under daily and unselfconscious circumstances.

Where you live will affect the number of choices you have for activities that will widen your social circle, but except in quite isolated rural communities there are more possibilities than you may realize. If you are politically minded, for example, you can volunteer to help at your local political club. Voluntary work for worthwhile causes, social service agencies, or nearby hospitals or schools may provide you with personal rewards at the same time that it brings you into contact with other people who share similar concerns. Those who like to be active and out of doors can seek out health clubs, hiking and biking clubs, wilderness, nature, and birdwatching groups.

If you can't find something that fits your particular taste, consider organizing it yourself. Any special interests can lead to social contacts. Musicians can start amateur chamber music groups, orchestras, or jazz, western, country, and ethnic music groups. Many towns and cities have amateur choirs, where an interest in singing is the only prerequisite. Painting, theater, handicraft, and folk art clubs are popular; if there is a Y in your community, you may find it is already sponsoring such activities. One midwestern woman started a sewing circle aimed specifically at men who wanted to learn how to quilt and do needlepoint. Organizing potluck dinners is a good way to cut costs and promote sociability. Cooking clubs are popular among both men and women. Woodworking and carpentry, wine making and tasting, chess and investment clubs, and bridge and other card and game clubs can be comfortable ways to meet people.

If you live in a city or its suburbs, you have the advantage of a wider choice of activities. Senior centers and community centers offer recreational opportunities; there are now over five thousand senior centers and clubs in the United States, operated by churches, synagogues, social clubs, and nonprofit corporations. These centers offer shows, parties, music, beauty salons, handicrafts, trips, discussion groups, and a variety of other things to do at the same time you are encountering new people.

Religious activities are another important way of meeting people. Many churches and synagogues sponsor singles clubs, and some are beginning to expand these to fit the needs of people in the mid and later years. Talk to your local cleric about starting such a group if one does not exist in your locale. If you are the parent of a child or an adolescent, Parents Without Partners clubs can be a source of contacts and of help to you, both as a parent and as a single person.

If you live in a rural area or a small town, you are more likely to know everyone who might be available as a friend or a companion in your area, just as they, in turn, know you. For variety you may want to make and visit friends in neighboring communities and get to larger urban areas for activities whenever possible. Trips and vacations away from home can be a way of making new acquaintances. If you don't have a car, arrange to share rides with others if you can. Neighbors and friends may be willing to serve as a taxi for you. Or you may be able to go by bus.

A small but growing number of older people have begun to live together in communal settings as a means of increasing their social contacts, cutting costs and sharing housekeeping duties. Some communes are made up only of older people, while others include people of all ages. Most of these are in large houses, although we have also heard of large apartments that are occupied communally and free of the chores of caring for a house and yard.

The two major organizations for older people, the National Council of Senior Citizens (national office at 925 15th Street, N.W., Washington, DC 20005) and the American Association of Retired Persons—National Retired Teachers Association (national office at 1909 K Street, N.W., Washington, DC 20006), may have chapters in your area where meetings of many kinds take place. Look in your phone book, or, if necessary, check with their national offices to see if there is a chapter near you. The AARP alone has twenty-seven million members, which provides for significant political advocacy and services (such as discount drugs, insurance coverage supplemental to Medicare, low-cost travel) as well as social opportunities. Widowed older people have been finding support and direction for their lives through the Widow to Widow program, which originated in Boston and is now being sponsored in other cities by the American Association of Retired Persons.

If you would like to combine opportunities for meeting people with social and political activism, the Gray Panthers (311 South Juniper Street, Philadelphia, PA 19107), which works vigorously on behalf of the older population, is adding local chapters rapidly, and includes younger as well as older people in its membership. The National Caucus on the Black Aged (2801 14th Street, N.W., 1st Floor, Washington, DC 20009) focuses on the problems of older black people.

Ocean cruises can be good fun and some people do meet partners this way, though they generally attract many more women than men and they are expensive. If you have the money, are interested in where you are going, and like to travel, you can enjoy yourself and make friends on a cruise. Don't be afraid to ask the ship's purser for help in meeting others and seating you with compatible dining companions. Younger men who are attracted to older women may use cruises as a meeting place, but be careful that they aren't interested chiefly in your money.

A more inexpensive way to travel sociably is to go on bus tours, some of which cover the entire United States and parts of Canada. You can get a ticket for use nationwide at reasonable rates. Take a friend, go by yourself or with a group, and be open to meeting new people along the way.

The travel industry is actively promoting travel for single people of all ages, with special seminars, tips for solo travelers, and special tour packages. Club Med [(800)528-3100], the Sierra Club trips [(415)981-8634], Smithsonian Associates tours [(202)287-3362], Lindblad Travel vacations (booked through travel agents), and Elderhostel programs (Suite 400, 80 Boylston Street, Boston, MA 02116) are popular with single people. Singleworld (booked through travel agents) offers worldwide cruises and tours for those traveling alone. Travel Companion Exchange [(516)454-0880] uses computerized listings to help pair single people for all sorts of travel, not just to arrange companions but to avoid the penalty many hotels, tours, and cruises place on single travelers.

Dance lessons are widely touted for older people, but be wary, because the commercial ones can be greatly overpriced and sometimes fraudulent, offering "lifetime contracts" and non-cancelable contracts. If you can't locate a reputable and reasonably priced place to learn, find friends who will teach you. If you are a good dancer, offer to teach someone else. Square dancing, folk, and ballroom dancing may bring back memories (as well as the dance steps themselves) from your past. A number of cities have relatively inexpensive public ballrooms; Roseland Dance City in New York, for example, has special matinees for older people. Friendships and romances can begin in such settings— Roseland has a plaque on its wall engraved with the names of married couples who first met there.

High school, college, and other reunions offer men and women the chance to renew acquaintance with compatible people they knew earlier in life, who are now widowed or divorced themselves. It is not uncommon for childhood sweethearts to meet again and even marry after each has raised a family and been widowed. Family reunions and family contacts in general are another way to get in touch with people who may be seeking new relationships; there is a long and honorable tradition, for example, of widows and widowers who are in-laws developing close relationships that end not infrequently in marriage or partnership at some level.

Commercial singles clubs and computer dating services are growing in popularity, especially for the young and middle-aged. But there is no reason why older people can't use them as well. Personal ads, too, have become popular and even reputable. For a small fee you can dream up a description of yourself and the kind of partner you are looking for and place it in the classified section of a wide variety of newspapers and magazines. Your identity is protected by a post office box number unless and until you choose to reveal yourself to a respondent.

If you are simply looking for an escort or temporary companion for a business or social event, there are legitimate agencies that will provide people, for a fee. Some escort services, however, are fronts for hiring sex partners (both male and female). If you are uneasy about commercial escort services, ask your local cleric whether he or she knows someone who could accompany you, or get in touch with an older-persons group or senior center.

Don't overlook born matchmakers among your friends, acquaintances, colleagues, your children, or other family members. Some people have highly developed sensibilities and can be very helpful in finding men or women you would enjoy meeting. But do save yourself time and trouble by picking your matchmaker carefully; look for someone whose judgment you respect and who knows you well.

Qualities That Foster New Relationships

It will help you in your first ventures into meeting new people if you remember that the men and women you encounter are as likely to be feeling tentative or somewhat shy as you are. Actually, you will find that what you look for in other people—as companions, as friends, as co-workers, or as intimates—are qualities they seek just as eagerly in you. Warmth and sensitivity to other people's feelings are greatly valued. One can be quiet or lively, according to one's temperament, as long as curiosity and an active mind underlie this temperament. Imagination, responsiveness, and a sense of humor are welcomed.

Certain personal qualities foster the art of companionship. Most people respond to a sense of vitality and energy. People who are pleasantly assertive (not domineering) have a greater chance of meeting new people and forming rewarding relationships, simply because they do not leave all the initiative up to others.

Qualities That Hinder New Relationships

It is important to maintain a positive approach that transcends or tempers any problems you have. We know from our clinical experience that certain personality features act as barriers to new relationships. Many older people have had much to endure through the deaths of spouses or friends, difficulties with children, financial burdens, and loneliness, and an increasing feeling of uselessness. Under these pressures, it is not uncommon to feel that life has been unfair and to bear a grudge against one's circumstances. But this resentment is likely to make other people wary of becoming involved with you. It is depressing to be with someone who is complaining or petulant and whose outlook is pessimistic. It takes a deliberate, conscious act of will to overcome the grim dependency on all that seems sour in one's life; but unless this is done, the chances for new and enriching relationships are diminished.

Can You Be Exploited?

Exploitation occurs in an emotional relationship when someone "uses" someone else without giving much in return. It is up to you to know what to look out for and how to protect yourself. Some older men (and, far more rarely, women) marry primarily to gain a housekeeper or nurse. The "romance" disappears as soon as the marriage vows are exchanged, and the woman discovers she has been recruited primarily to perform services. It is much wiser, of course, to take time to learn as much as you can about the other person before you decide to marry. The history of his or her relationships with the opposite sex can be illuminating. Most exploiters have a long history of taking advantage of others.

At other times the exploiter may be after your money or property. Matrimonial swindles through lonely-hearts clubs and correspondence with strangers who claim a romantic interest in you are notorious. The tip-off comes when the person begins to be inordinately interested in your property, your money, or your will. If you suspect this is happening to you, get to a lawyer, cleric, or someone else you can trust, and ask for advice.

Special Problems for Women

Unattached older women, especially those who are widowed or divorced, often find themselves left out of activities that involve couples. Hostesses at dinner parties feel they must have a man available for each woman guest, with couples coming two by two like the creatures on Noah's Ark. The hostess may also find the presence of a widow or divorcee uncomfortable, fearing possible competition.

If you are frequently left out socially, one solution is to join with other single people and organize your own activities. Develop a circle of friends in which friendship rather than gender is the key to getting together, and make these times occasions where people of any age or marital status and either sex can enjoy one another's company. Your married friends can also be invited, and in the process may become less inflexible about their own social habits in inviting guests.

If you are a divorced woman, be prepared to have some people see you as a failure; they make the conscious or unconscious assumption that the breakup of your marriage was caused by a flaw in you. Talk this over with understanding people who care about you.

Both widows and divorcees find that some men (married or otherwise) assume that women who are sexually experienced are automatically available and willing. Indeed, these men may see themselves as doing you a sexual favor. If this annoys or upsets you, simply tell them so.

Special Problems for Men

As a general rule, unattached men have fewer *social* difficulties. Even those who had not thought themselves socially very accomplished when they were younger may be surprised to find how eagerly accepted and actively pursued they now are. This is largely because there are fewer men than women; and a man who enjoys relationships with women is likely to have ample opportunity for them. On the other hand, if you are a man who finds it annoying or troubling to be treated like a commodity in short supply, you will have to make this clear or else remove yourself from those situations where this tends to occur.

Uncertainty can be a problem for men. Many men, like many women, are hesitant, shy, or dubious about their ability to handle personal relationships. To find yourself valued as an available man as you grow older is not automatically reassuring if you doubt your sophistication, skill, or appeal to the opposite sex. Most men have been conditioned to believe that anything short of total self-confidence is shameful, a failure of "masculinity." Though a woman may have similar problems of self-confidence, society has not pressured her into feeling "unwomanly" as a result. Any man troubled by doubts about his skill in social and sexual situations should know that he has plenty of company, and that this is no reflection on his manliness. He should also remember that most women he meets are not going to measure him against some impossible ideal and judge him a failure. Further, the man who is shy, diffident, or uncertain about his competence will have to make the same effort of will, and exercise the same degree of initiative, that a hesitant woman must undertake. Without this determination relationships will not just happen for him any more than for her.

As a Relationship Develops

New anxieties may occur as a relationship progresses to sexual involvement. When men or women doubt their sexual performance, or fear that the person with whom they are involved may be measuring them against the behavior of a previous partner, it will affect sexual ability. It takes an active effort by both concerned to make the present moment satisfying. Memories of past lovemaking should not be allowed to dominate the present. What each of you can give the other should concern you more than anything else. A caring person who offers reassurance to a partner who is feeling uncertain about his or her skill will help restore confidence. Sexual problems with deep roots may require professional help, but the self-doubt that has its roots in shyness and uneasiness about performance—which is much more common—is often alleviated by thoughtfulness and tenderness.

Handling Refusals, Rebuffs, and Disappointments

However confident they may appear on the surface, a great many men and women worry about rebuffs when they initiate or respond to a social opportunity. How can you handle refusals and disappointments? It is natural to feel hurt, but you should not let this feeling persist. You have to accept the possibility of rejection whenever you involve yourself with others, so be matter-of-fact about it. It is, after all, the other person's right—as it is yours when you are approached. It should not deter you from further involvements. Rejection actually serves a very practical function by keeping people apart who would probably be unhappy together.

Obviously, there will be some occasions when the rebuff is rude and takes no account of your feelings. Inevitably, a certain proportion of your social contacts will prove to be unpleasant, and sometimes even painful. This is unavoidable in human relationships at any age. The point to remember is that refusals or disappointments do not mean you are a failure as a person. If you are losing confidence and feel you need a fresh perspective on yourself, talk over your experiences with a close friend. Then try again. Draw on the experience you have gained even from the unpleasant event. Take a few chances. Above all, do not waste time berating yourself for what does not work out. Learn to assess wisely the difference between what is your responsibility and that which is beyond your control.

Moving Too Fast

What if one partner in a newly acquainted couple moves too quickly toward intimacy? Many older people dread the thought of the widow who is husband-hunting or the man who is on the make sexually on the first date. Use your common sense. Don't be afraid to tell the other person if you are feeling pushed. Be sensitive to your companion's feelings, especially if you yourself are an impulsive or action-oriented individual. A relationship that is going to be more than merely temporary needs time to build. People must explore each other's feelings and learn more about each other. Decide together what pace to set. Many people are not ready for physical intimacies—much less marriage—until they feel a mutual understanding and affection. An enduring partnership is based on thoughtfulness as well as attraction.

Arranging for Privacy When You Live With Your Children

Living with your children, as roughly 20 percent of older people do, can put a damper on your social life unless you take steps to prevent it. Don't depend on your children to recognize your needs for privacy. You will need to take the initiative and discuss this with them frankly. Work out ways of sharing the space available in the home, so that there will be times when you can entertain people privately. Some houses are large enough for you to have your own suite of rooms, which makes a separate social life easier. But most older people will have a bedroom at most, and sometimes even this will have to be shared with another member of the family. If you have your own room and it is a reasonable size, you can furnish it as a combination bedroom–sitting room and entertain your friends there. If small children live in the house, a lock or latch on the door will keep them from running in and out until they learn to knock and enter only on invitation. Your bed can be a couch by day, and you should also have a comfortable chair and other amenities for entertaining. If you must share a bedroom, arrange to have sole use of the room at certain times. There may be difficulties in entertaining privately in the family living or dining room unless you and your family have worked out a practical schedule. It is easier if there is also a recreation room or den. If your resources permit, you might want to help finance the construction of additional space or undertake some remodeling.

It is extremely important that you make your children aware of your desire for privacy *before* you move in with them. Discussing the issue before actual situations arise is more likely to produce results. When it is they who are moving in with you, things are usually a bit easier because you are on your own territory to begin with. The crucial element in living successfully with one's children is to be able to talk openly with them about problems and cooperate in solving them.

Affairs and Living Together

Many couples who come to care for each other want to marry, because marriage confirms for them the permanence and depth of their commitment. For some older people, in addition, the idea of living together without marriage goes against moral or religious scruples. But the number of unmarried men and women of all ages living together as sexual partners has more than tripled since 1970, with nearly two million such households in 1984. Much publicity has been given to this phenomenon as it affects the young and the middle-aged. Less is known about older persons who live together. Perhaps a much larger number live separately but have affairs. The decision a couple makes may involve deliberate choice or may be the result of necessity. Two people may care deeply for each other but feel that marriage would set limits on an independence they have come to value. We have known older men and women who nursed partners through long chronic illness until death, and who felt that they did not want to enter into another marriage that might put them through the same ordeal again.

There are also instances in which marriage is not possible. Eveyone knows of unhappy marriages that continue for years because one partner will not agree to divorce, forcing the other to seek a partner outside marriage. In other marriages, one member may have been incapacitated or chronically ill for a long time, leaving the other without a satisfying sexual and emotional outlet. Outside relationships are more likely if the marital couple had an unsatisfying emotional relationship to begin with, or if one partner is mentally impaired or institutionalized. Sometimes the children of a widowed parent object strongly to his or her remarriage, and the parent does not wish to cause family conflict.

Economic factors may also enter into decisions not to remarry. There may be pension penalties for remarriage. Recent legislation has improved this situation somewhat, but penalties still remain. State Medicaid benefits can also be a barrier to remarriage. If one partner has been receiving Medicaid, marriage would mean suspending that support until the entire savings of the new spouse was used up; only then could Medicaid be resumed. Indeed, there have been cases where husband and wife divorced each other, though continuing to live together, in order for one of them to be eligible for Medicaid.

In general, the decision of whether to marry or simply to live together is a private one, to be reached by each individual couple. There can be many inducements on both sides, including religious attitudes, the reactions of relatives, financial considerations, and personal preferences. Couples must find the solution that best suits their circumstances.

Chapter 8

Learning New Patterns of Lovemaking

*I*f you have been thinking about some aspects of your sex life that you would like to alter, now is the time to do it. Don't believe people who tell you that as you grow older you cannot help becoming too fixed in your ways to change. If yours was the kind of temperament interested in learning and changing earlier, it is likely to remain so all your life. Scientific studies have proved beyond question that older people can learn as well as and in some cases better than the young.

But do not underestimate the strength of habit, which is all the more powerful for being unconscious: lovemaking patterns tend to become fixed and uninspired over the years, often because you have neither taken the time nor thought it necessary to examine them. Do you always make love at the same time of day and in the same manner? Are you excited and interested in your love life? Do your partner and you know how to please each other? It may be time to loosen up, try something new, and learn to relish once again the special warmth and intimacy that are possible through love and sex.

The Setting for Sex

Look at your bedroom with a critical eye. Is it comfortable and pleasant? Is it a good place for sex? A firm, comfortable bed for two is standard equipment unless illness, sleeping problems, or personal preference lead you to choose single beds. The best arrangement in this case is one double bed for making love, talking, and other intimacies, with a single bed in the same room or another room when you are ready to separate for sleep. A double bed encourages the closeness and sharing that enrich a couple's sense of togetherness.

Many older people develop the habit of lining up their medications on their bed stands. This is aesthetically unattractive and a dangerous practice as well. People in a drowsy condition may fail to read labels, take the wrong pills in the middle of the night, or accidentally take too many. We recommend that all medications be placed out of sight at a walking distance from the bed unless they are absolutely essential for emergencies (for example, nitroglycerin for those with heart problems). In addition to protecting yourself, you will not be continually confronting yourself and your partner with reminders of your pains or infirmities.

Another thing that has struck us about many older people's bedrooms is the gallery of family pictures—children, grandchildren, nephews, nieces, and ancestors—that often lines the walls. This is fine for a couple married for many years, who feel comfortable in this setting. But it can be unnerving, to say the least, for a new partner to settle down expectantly in the bed and find your relatives looking down on the proceedings. Be sensitive to your new partner's feelings. If family pictures are interfering with your love life, banish them to another room.

The Time for Sex

Finding the best time for sexual activity can enhance a sexual relationship. Sex exclusively at bedtime is an easy habit to get into over the years, when daytime privacy is hard to come by and the pressures of work and family crowd your days. Yet this may not really be your favorite time. And after the age of sixty, it may not be your most energetic period either. Overstressed and overworked couples, particularly, may need to set aside several evenings a week to make a date with each other, relax, and go to bed early, before exhaustion sets in. Some couples sleep first and make love in the morning. Others wake each other in the middle of the night, when both have had some rest. Many men report greater sexual potency after a good night's sleep. The morning is a favorite time for many older people because they are rested and relaxed. Naps when possible during the day can make for greater vigor in the evening for those who prefer nighttime lovemaking out of choice rather than by default. Experimenting with new times on weekends, holidays, and vacations can be invigorating. When vacations away from home are not possible, take a vacation at home. If you have the house to yourself, unplug the phone and let the outside world know you're not available.

Learning how to relax is also a useful skill. A warm bath or shower before sex can relax you in a pleasant manner. Exchanging massages with your partner, turning the lights low, and listening to music can also help you unwind. (Massage courses for couples are now available in many major cities as part of adult education programs.) A *small* glass of an alcoholic beverage can be a tension reliever—we recommend dry white wine or warm Japanese sake. Warm milk, although not the world's sexiest drink, can bring relaxation.

What You Can Do for Your Partner

We are not going to describe the extensive technical knowledge that people can acquire about how to make love. This has been described adequately in other books (see Bibliography for examples), and in our opinion the technique of sex has been overemphasized, giving lovemaking more the character of a gymnastic workout or hard labor than the expression of love. This is not to say that, through reading and other methods, you cannot learn much that is valuable; but always remember that, although skill can enhance the communication of genuine warmth and affection, it can never substitute for them or take primacy.

We do want to direct your attention to information that is especially relevant to older people. For older women, the most common sexual problem is the inability to achieve orgasm. "Frigidity" is the word often used to describe this situation, and it is an unfortunate term because it implies coldness and sexual indifference. This does not adequately explain what happens to many women.

There are periods in the sexual lives of most women when they do not experience orgasm, but this is usually transient. Temporary loss of reponse can have many causes, among them tiredness, emotional upset, boredom, vaginal infections or other physical ailments, drugs, and lack of adequate stimulation of the clitoris. In addition, numbers of women never attain orgasm through intercourse but can reach it through other means, such as petting or self-stimulation. Orgasm by any of these means can be enjoyable. Others do not have orgasms through any method, including masturbation. Severe or total lack of sexual response that is ongoing can usually be traced to emotional attitudes developed during the early years of life. For some women this is extremely troubling; for others mildly so; and the remainder do not consider it to be a problem.

There is growing evidence that women may have a different view of sexuality from men, placing less importance on the act of sexual intercourse itself and more on the physical cuddling and personal warmth, talking, and sharing that may surround a sexual relationship. While there's no indication that women are less interested than men in achieving orgasm and sexual release, many prefer sexual activities other than, or in addition to, intercourse. Female anatomy plays an important role in women's attitudes. The majority of women receive their primary sexual satisfaction from clitoral stimulation, and that direct or indirect clitoral stimulation is the initial requirement in the production of female orgasm. Because of this, sexual intercourse is often not satisfying unless it involves direct, manual stimulation of the clitoris. (A number of studies indicate that substantially fewer women achieve orgasm regularly through sexual intercourse than through other methods.) Men can learn to stimulate the clitoral area, whether by hand, mouth, or by the penis itself, and women should tell them what is pleasurable and what is not. Finally, some older women have problems of lubrication and may require longer periods of sex play before lubrication actually begins. K-Y jelly can be placed in the vagina if lubrication is insufficient.

Women can learn to be sensitive and helpful when men are having problems with impotence. Try a new coital position by bending your knees and placing a pillow under your hips to elevate your pelvis, in order to more easily accommodate your partner's partially erect penis. Remember that erection can be stimulated by touching the penis, so learn to massage it. Do not pull it up toward the abdomen, where it will lose blood. Instead, push down, with pressure at the base of the penis, which will put pressure on major blood vessels to hold the blood that the penis already contains.

A woman can further the strength of an erection by literally stuffing the partially erect penis into her vagina and flexing her vaginal muscles until it achieves full erection. Many women like to hold the penis in their vagina after lovemaking. If they have developed their vaginal muscles, this may be possible even if the penis begins to become limp, as happens more quickly after orgasm as men grow older. Finally, we want to stress again that a women need not feel obligated to "give a man an orgasm"every time they make love. Leave this up to the man to decide and concentrate on mutually enjoying the physical and emotional contact, as well as your own orgasm if it occurs.

Men and women can learn to accommodate each other's needs in other ways. If one of you is obese or has a protruding abdomen, for example, you will need to experiment to find a sexual position that allows the penis to reach the vagina. (Naturally you should also be dieting!) The triangle technique can be used, in which the woman lies on her back with legs apart and knees sharply bent, while the man places himself over her with his hips under the angle formed by her raised knees. Another accessible position is for the man to lie on his back while the woman sits astride him.

Today older people experiment more with various sexual positions, just as do the young. There are many alternatives to the standard "missionary" position of the woman underneath, on her back, and the man on top. The most common ones are lying side by side; the woman on top; or the man entering the woman from the rear.

As we have indicated, there are also a number of satisfying sexual alternatives to intercourse. These include mutual stimulation of each other's genitals by hand as well as stimulation of other erotic areas of the body—the mouth, neck, ears, breasts, and buttocks. Some couples use these techniques as foreplay before intercourse. Others use them as substitutes, either because intercourse is not possible or because they prefer them.

Sex gadgets are generally a waste of money except for battery-driven vibrators, which many people find stimulating, and certain prosthetic devices, which can help a man maintain a rigid penis or which can substitute completely for one. Older women should avoid douching after sex with perfumed douches or using vaginal sprays now widely sold. They are unnecessary and can cause medical problems.

Solo Sex

Self-stimulation, or masturbation, is a common and healthy practice that usually begins in childhood. It is natural for all children to explore their bodies, and most children stimulate themselves sexually unless they are prevented by adults from doing so. There is evidence that self-stimulation is an important preliminary to adult sexuality, enabling people to learn to recognize and satisfy their sexual feelings. The Kinsey studies of 1948–50 found that 92 percent of men and 62 percent of women had masturbated at some time in their life, and indications are that masturbation has increased in women. The 1982 Merck Manual, a highly reputable source of medical information, reports that approximately 97 percent of males and 80 percent of females have masturbated at some point in their lives. The Hite Report of 1976 found that 82 percent of all women masturbate, and all but 5 percent have orgasms while doing so. The evidence seems clear that, although masturbation was once seen as a perversion and a cause of mental and physical disease, it is now recognized as a normal sexual activity throughout life.

Self-stimulation provides a sexual outlet for people—unmarried, widowed, or divorced—who do not have partners, as well as for husbands or wives whose partners are ill or away. Some people practice self-stimulation in addition to sexual intercourse, particularly if they prefer sex more frequently than their partner does or enjoy the variety masturbation affords. As described earlier, many women experience more intense and more frequent orgasms through mutual or self-masturbation than during intercourse. Masturbation can continue until very late in life and has been reported by some men in their nineties. A 1983 Consumer Union survey found that 66 percent of men and 47 percent of women in their fifties masturbate with some regularity; over the age of seventy, 43 percent of men and 33 percent of women still masturbate. Some people begin to masturbate for the first time after they grow older, particularly if they have no partner or become too physically incapacitated for intercourse.

Total abstinence from sexual activity over a long period of time can be tension-producing and may result in potency problems in men and loss of lubrication as well as vaginal shape in women. It can be beneficial to free yourself from the notion that self-stimulation is unhealthy, immoral, or immature. A source of pleasure to be learned and enjoyed for its own sake, masturbation also resolves sexual tensions, keeps sexual desire alive, is good physical exercise, and helps to preserve sexual functioning in both men and women who have no other outlets. Vibrators can be useful aids in masturbation. Many people have sexual fantasies, which add to the pleasure of self-stimulation.

Communicating With Your Partner About Sex

Partners often find it helpful to talk with each other about their sexual feelings. Embarrassment and feelings of awkwardness are common at first. In addition, many couples first assume that they don't have to talk, since sex "comes naturally." But this simply is not accurate. Because people are all different, with unique likes and dislikes, it is naive to assume that our partners can read our minds or know intuitively how to please us. Furthermore, it is often said that sex begins in the brain, by the stimulation of the imagination and by memory of previous sexual experience. Our mind may well be our most sensitive and reliable organ of sensuality.

Begin by discussing your feelings about talking about sex. Then help each other by telling your partner what gives you pleasure. Finally, try in every way possible to do what is pleasurable for each other. You may be surprised at what you don't know about your partner and what you may have been reluctant to admit about yourself. You can also reminisce, talking about your first memories of sex, your early sexual attitudes and those of your family, and perhaps your feelings about what it means to be a man or a woman. Compare notes on what you would most like to change about yourself and your partner sexually. Be thoughtful and kind about the way you express any dissatisfactions you may feel. Do not hesitate to express your warmth and affection when these are honestly felt.

Some couples share their sexual fantasies with each other. Such fantasies, which are part of most people's sex lives, involve any visual and sexually stimulating images one conjures up. Some people are excited by imagining forbidden or unavailable sex partners, settings, or practices. Others bring to mind sexual experiences from the past that have been especially exciting. Some couples make up fantasies for each other. Recently couples have begun reporting the use of videocassette tapes in their home to enhance fantasy and sexual stimulation.

The value of fantasy is that it adds a new dimension to one's sex life as well as acting as a substitute, rather like an auxiliary motor, if something is not going well. People who may be otherwise fond of their partners but not easily aroused by them as years go by report that fantasies, including fantasies of their partners and themselves when they were younger ("fantasy reruns"), can often get things started and help in reaching climax. Fantasy may be used to override a physical disability or distract a person from anxiety or other preoccupations. Mental imagining can be especially useful for persons whose vision is impaired. Since poor vision can interfere with the vital transfer of visual stimuli into sexual arousal, fantasy may be a means of recapturing such stimuli.

So far we have few useful studies about fantasy in mid and later life. It would be interesting, for example, to know whether people usually fantasize themselves and others as younger than their actual ages.

Books on sexuality and emotional relationships can help couples learn more about themselves and each other. It is useful and stimulating to take a fresh look from time to time at what you know about sexuality and at the current attitudes of society toward sex. We have recommended a number of books in the Bibliography. There are many more, although most of them assume a young and middle-aged readership. Therefore a book such as *Sex: A User's Manual* (G. P. Putnam's Sons, 1981) is unusual in presenting a separate section on sexuality and aging. Films and tapes that are specifically addressed to medical and other aspects of sexuality in the mid and later years are becoming available to both professionals in health care and the public.

Chapter 9

Dating, Remarriage, and Your Children

O ur patient files contain many examples of conflicts between parents and their adult children that develop when a parent is widowed (or divorced) and attempts to build a new life through dating and, possibly, remarriage: "My daughter doesn't like my fiancée and thinks she is only interested in my money." "My son Jim feels I'd be a fool to marry Harry, that Harry has always been a ladies' man." "My children think I'm crazy to want a man. I wouldn't dare tell them what I did on my cruise to Jamaica."

Not all children create problems. Many are pleased at the thought of their parents leading full and satisfying lives. Others have realistic worries about practical implications; they may welcome the remarriage of a father to a somewhat younger woman, because she will be able to nurse him as he grows older, but may feel threatened if their mother marries an older man, because it will be a burden on her and potentially on them if he falls ill.

For still other children the reactions are entirely emotional. The thought of a parent becoming involved with a new partner can provoke anxiety, threat, jealousy, hurt, anger, or grief. They may be strongly inclined to offer unasked-for advice and even to take over if they feel a parent is making a mistake. Coercion, threats, and angry withdrawal are not uncommon.

There are numerous reasons why adult children react so negatively. Those who never became fully independent psychologically will use their parents to fulfill emotional needs that should be met by their partners and friends. This can be assumed if your child acts possessive or personally aggrieved when you become involved in a relationship, not unlike a wounded lover. It is possible that you yourself (perhaps unconsciously) have encouraged an inappropriately close relationship with this child, or that other circumstances have kept the child from emancipating him- or herself. Age is not a factor in these situations. Your fifty-year-old child can be dependent in this way even though he or she is married and has children. Under these circumstances, the best approach is to let your children know, kindly but definitely, that you intend to lead your own life, and to encourage them to do likewise.

Sometimes parents find that their children harbor the ignorance and misinformation about sex in later life that we have discussed in earlier chapters. They cling to the parental image of you only as Mom or Dad and do not recognize or want to recognize that you need sex and love just as they do. It is probable that you have encouraged this yourself by playing only the parent role whenever you were around them. A good antidote is to tell them more about your social interests and to bring your friends and dates home to meet them. You can still retain your privacy, but they should become aware that you are entitled to emotional and personal commitments. Though they may never feel entirely at ease about your right to a sexually satisfying life, they can often be helped to come to terms with its reality.

Children will sometimes try to preserve the memory of their deceased parent (or your former relationship with a divorced spouse) by the process of *enshrinement,* discussed earlier in terms of widowhood. They maintain a fierce reverence for the past and want to see nothing changed, so they consider any new relationships you enter into an affront to their other parent. You can then find yourself accused of being selfish, insensitive, or disloyal; and if they succeed in making you feel guilty, you may be compelled to sever your new relationship. This is a mistake. Your children need to work through their own anger and grief at the death (or divorce) that ended your marriage. They are often bound to the past by a mixture of positive and negative feelings, and it is this ambivalence that must be resolved. Talk to them freely about their feelings, listen to their reactions, and try honestly to answer questions and clarify confusion. Let them know, also, how you have handled your own feelings about their other parent.

Another problem can develop if your children hold grievances and grudges against you, which they demonstrate by refusing to condone your right to build a new life for yourself. Some of these grievances may be lifelong, others recent; some may be misconceptions and misunderstandings of your actions toward them, particularly during their childhood, and others may be legitimate. Adult children may become critical of their parents because their parents were always critical of them. Others remember being harshly punished or humiliated for innocent sexual experiences in childhood and have grown up thinking sex is wrong or dirty, the sex lives of their parents included. If you can begin listening openly to their grievances—and it may be difficult—there is a chance that you and your children can develop a new understanding and respect for each other. Be ready to admit where you may have failed; but don't take the blame for everything. Your children and your former partner played their roles too. The point is not to pin down a culprit, find a "bad guy," or allay grievances by making yourself a martyr, but to clarify what happened, why it happened, and whether anything can now be done to build a better relationship. Frank talk itself sometimes heals old wounds. And when it doesn't, *you* decide what choice you are going to make.

Next we must look at a problem that can terrorize a parent— the spoiled child. This is the child who grows up believing himself or herself to be inordinately important and never stops believing it. Every spoiled child has one and usually two parents who were easily intimidated, overindulgent, or lax with discipline. A favorite tactic of such a child is to threaten to withdraw love if the parent does not cater to his or her wishes. This tactic is all the more devastating when the child grows to middle age and attains greater power as the parent becomes older and loses status and authority. The sooner you get a grip on this situation, the better. Do not let your son or daughter dictate to you. It isn't good for you, and it isn't good for your child. It may be frightening to think of losing this love, but remember that children rarely "divorce" their parents, at least not for long, and particularly if they know basically that you care about them.

Spoiled children have an intuitive understanding of power since they learned to use it expertly at a very early age. Use power in your turn, to let them know the score. First of all, *keep your grip on your own money and property.* Then start making a few of your own decisions, particularly about your personal life. Get outside authority figures to help you if you need them in the initial battles that are bound to come. Your lawyer, cleric, or a respected friend or family member may be able to support you when you waver, or speak for you if at first you can't. You can be heartened by the knowledge that spoiled children usually develop respect for people who refuse to be manipulated.

Finally, we come to a most painful problem, the will-watching child—found particularly in those families where there will be a sizable estate after a parent's death. This child is forever worrying about his or her share of your estate and casts a cold eye on anyone you may be dating or thinking of marrying. Such a child will often plant suspicions in your mind that any close friend or prospective mate is after whatever money you have. Older people can be and have been exploited, of course, but if your mind is sound, you should rely on your own judgment and perhaps that of trusted friends or advisers—and *not* on a child with a family reputation for overconcern about money or an inclination to avarice. (If you begin to have any question about your own judgment, you can seek legal advice to set up a conservatorship. This will protect you, your funds, and your estate.)

What makes a child obsessive about his or her inheritance? Many things: parental overindulgence, feelings of being unloved, a long-standing family overemphasis on money, or lack of training in the pleasure there is in generosity and sharing with others. Simple selfishness and greed also exist. This is a difficult problem to rectify unless your child is motivated to discover the basis of his or her attitudes toward material possessions. You can try to understand any part you may have played in shaping these attitudes and see what changes in them you can make. But also protect yourself financially and emotionally from capitulating to your child's demands. Your estate is your own to disperse as you see fit. If your son or daughter puts the pressure on, it may help to keep the provisions of your will secret. If the child is capable of maintaining some rationality in this area, however, it may be helpful to say exactly what you intend to do so that he or she can learn to live with it. The important thing is to be decisive and remain unintimidated by veiled or open threats, pressures, and pleadings focused upon your property.

In general, your children's emotional reactions toward your personal life are likely to run deep and require your special attention if you are to avoid unnecessary alienation and hostility. Family councils and heart-to-heart talks can help enormously. But if all else fails, look for professional advice and try to get your children to join you. If they refuse, seek help by yourself, but make it clear to your children (and to yourself) that you are working toward their eventual acceptance of your new life.

Premarital Legal Planning

Premarital legal planning is advisable and often essential. We will focus on only one important form of such planning, the premarital agreement or contract, also called a prenuptial or antenuptial agreement and not to be confused with modern marriage contracts, which stipulate marital duties and are not legally binding. Premarital agreements deal only with money and other property. Alternative forms (trusts, for example) should also be considered but are beyond the scope of this book. Whatever kind of premarital planning you elect will require the consultation of a lawyer.

There are many parents who want to leave at least part of their estate directly to their children and are concerned about the effects of remarriage on this intention. If you are planning to remarry and want to make special financial arrangements for the benefit of your children or any other persons, you and your spouse-to-be can work out a premarital agreement. In most states these agreements are a time-honored method for allaying the fears of children and planning one's estate wisely and in their best interests. Such agreements also protect older people themselves, by keeping their resources intact and unavailable to anyone but designated persons. Wealthy people have traditionally used premarital agreements for marriages at any age, in order to protect family estates. Now that people live longer, with more late-life marriages and with more extensive estates to dispose of, premarital agreements are increasingly common. The agreement customarily describes what will *not* be available to the prospective spouse.

To be legally enforceable, such an agreement must be in writing, by reason of the Statute of Frauds in force in all states. The Uniform Premarital Agreement Act, approved by the Bar Association in February 1984, can be used as a model for a premarital agreement. As a basic agreement acceptable in all states, it is likely to stand up in court.

How does a premarital agreement work? Let's take a couple who plan to marry, each of whom has been widowed and has children. The premarital agreement enables them to plan their respective estates in the way that suits them. The advantage to the children lies in the fact that their parent's new spouse will receive an amount less than ordinary under the Statute of Descent and Distributions and the children will receive more. An added advantage is that under such an agreement the children will receive somewhat more than if the parent had died intestate (without a will).

A premarital agreement is different from a will. It is a waiver to the right of the spouse to a certain minimum claim to your property at death. A will can be changed at any time without the spouse's knowledge or consent, while a premarital agreement can be amended only with the consent of both parties. It is binding as of the time of the marriage, whereas a will goes into effect only at the time of death. A will can, of course, be changed to give a spouse more and the children less than the premarital agreement stated. But unless the will stipulates this, the spouse cannot lay claim to any more than the premarital agreement provides.

People may find premarital agreements useful even though their estates are small. An illustration might be the widower of moderate assets with children by his first wife, who had assisted him in earning the money he has accumulated and whose children contributed actively as well. Now that he wants to remarry, there is some resentment on the part of the children that the new bride will be automatically entitled to one-third (or whatever proportion is operative in a particular state) of their father's entire estate in the event of his death. If he chooses to do so, the father can decide on a premarital agreement that provides something less than one-third of the estate for the new wife, with the rest going to children or grandchildren. The financial gain to the children may be small, but emotionally it may mean a great deal.

There are situations where premarital agreements have been challenged, and the courts have in some cases upheld those challenges if fraud was involved or certain formalities had not been observed. The law says that the contracting parties must be in a confidential (or fiduciary) relationship to each other, meaning that there must be a good-faith disclosure of assets. For example, the failure of a man to reveal that he has several hundred thousand dollars (who tells his bride-to-be that he has only $20,000 so that she agrees to take the sum of $5,000 in the event of his death) makes the agreement subject to challenge on the basis of fraud.

Another problem is separation or divorce. Premarital agreements provide for the eventuality of death, and these agreements are expressly recognized in about one-fourth of the states by statute and in most of the other states by judicial decision. When the agreement deals not only with the division of property in the event of death, but with the possibility of divorce as well, problems may be encountered. For example, many states hold that agreements entered into before marriage to provide for divorce payments in the event of separation are invalid. However, a Washington, DC, District Court of Appeals decision (*Burtoff* v. *Burtoff*) upheld this broadening of a premarital agreement as it related to alimony and property settlements.

How much should you tell your children about your premarital agreement, or the making or changing of your will? Some parents inform each child fully or have their lawyer do so. Others give a general picture but not the specifics. Still others keep everything totally secret. What you do depends on your own judgment. Children may be relieved to have at least a general idea of your intentions. But if privacy about your own financial affairs is important to you, you have every right to keep your arrangements to yourself.

Chapter 10

Where to Go for Help

We have discussed what older people can do for themselves to understand and remedy sexual, personal, and social problems. But when such problems persist, outside professional help may be a good idea.

A thorough evaluation is crucial to determining exactly where the problem lies. The first step in any evaluation of sexual problems in this age group should *always* be a medical examination. Physical problems can cause serious sexual difficulties by themselves, or they can team up with emotional or social problems to create a baffling group of sexual symptoms. Unraveling the medical aspects of sexual problems may be quite simple or terribly complicated, but it cannot be neglected.

Finding Medical Help

How do you find a doctor who is knowledgeable about sex? How do you find one who is interested in older people and understands the special problems of sex in later life? Frankly, it may be difficult. Many doctors—those graduating from medical school before 1961—have not had sex education as part of their medical school training. This has slowly changed, but you will still find that many doctors are surprisingly unenlightened and embarrassed to talk about sexual activity throughout the course of the life cycle. Many draw primarily upon their own personal sexual philosophy and experience. This is especially true about sex in the later years. They may also personally share the culture's negative attitude toward old age. It is not uncommon for women past fifty to find that their doctor begins to "forget" to do a thorough gynecological exam during a routine physical examination.

Adding to the difficulty of a search for a sympathetic and knowledgeable doctor is the fact that most doctors have not had systematic training in the general medical problems of older people. This also is slowly changing and some medical school programs have begun to include geriatrics—the study of old age—in their curricula, but lack of knowledge and interest remains widespread among practicing physicians. Two national organizations, the American Geriatrics Society (770 Lexington Avenue, Suite 400, New York, NY 10021), and the Gerontological Society's Clinical Medicine Section (1411 K Street, N.W., Suite 300, Washington, DC 20005) may be able to help you locate doctors in your area who are knowledgeable in geriatrics. You can also write the Office of Information of the National Institute on Aging (National Institutes of Health, Bethesda, MD 20205) or the National Institute of Mental Health (National Institutes of Health, Rockville, MD 20857) for a list of doctors or clinics specializing in geriatrics and gerontology arranged by geographical area.

Remember, however, that there is an extremely small percentage of doctors active in this field. It is also true that membership in these organizations does not guarantee competence in the field of aging, and individual doctors who are not specialists in the field may be equally sensitive and knowledgeable in working with older people. An able and understanding general practitioner or internist who takes care of patients of all ages can serve you very well indeed. If you are lucky, your own doctor may be such a person. Some people, of course, feel more comfortable talking about sexual problems with a new doctor who is a total stranger, and if this is the case with you, by all means do so. The main point is to go to a doctor with whom you feel as relaxed as possible and whom you trust to be both medically competent and generally receptive toward older people.

What else can you do? You owe it to yourself to learn how to give proper information and ask the right questions, and thus encourage your doctor to take your sexual problems seriously. It may be embarrassing to talk about what is on your mind. Don't let that stop you. Your experiences and problems are shared by many older people. Tell the doctor exactly what you are worried about. Include any detail that you think might be helpful in evaluating the symptoms. Older women may feel reluctant to describe sexual problems in general, or problems in the vaginal area in particular, especially to a male doctor. Older men may not want to admit problems with potency. But this is false modesty and false pride. Candid talk will go a long way toward making it easier to diagnose and treat your problem.

There are a number of things you should look for as you work with doctors:

▸ Watch out for doctors who quickly dismiss your sexual concern with such comments as "What do you expect at your age?" "Go home and take a cold shower," "Stop worrying," "Nothing can be done." Persist in your desire for help, and if the doctor continues to be unresponsive, find a new doctor.

▸ Expect the doctor to take a good medical history, which includes a review of the body's systems and functions as well as a history of present and past illnesses. Specifically, the doctor should ask you about any changes you have observed in your genital organs, including in men any bowing of the penis and in women stress incontinence.

▸ Be aware that not only do diseases affect sexuality but the proper control of disease may restore good sexual functioning in many instances.

▸ Expect the doctor to take a thorough sexual and marital history as well as a medical history. Questions are likely to cover the ways you and your partner feel about sex, its frequency and pleasure, and any disagreements you may have. The doctor will also explore the impact of attitudes toward sex you may have developed in childhood. You will find it valuable to share with your doctor the history of sexual experiences you may have had with other people at other times. Male patients should be asked if they have problems with urination and with achieving and holding erections. They should be questioned as to whether they ever have erections as they wake up in the morning. Females should be questioned carefully as to whether they are having any pain during intercourse or any unusual soreness or bleeding.

▶ The doctor should ask what drugs you are taking, both prescription and over-the-counter, and be able to explain the sexual side effects of each drug. It is sometimes possible to switch to equally effective drugs with fewer sexual side effects.

▶ If you have already had surgery on any sex organs, the doctor should be able to tell you if this is in any way affecting your sexuality. If surgery is planned, learn in advance any possible sexual consequences. Do not be embarrassed to ask specific questions about anything that is troubling you.

▶ Discuss with your doctor a program of preventive health care. This should include attention to smoking, drinking, nutrition, exercise, rest, stress, and emotional problems.

▶ Using these questions and the doctor's reactions to you as a guide, and relying as well on your own common sense, if you feel your doctor's examination has been insufficient, talk to him or her openly about your misgivings. As a patient, you are entitled to satisfaction.

▶ Finally, your doctor should ask if you have any questions.

After the medical examination it should be fairly clear whether physical problems are the sole or, more likely, the partial cause of symptoms of sexual dysfunction and whether medical treatment is indicated. In the majority of cases, the medical examination is likely to show that bodily changes are not involved significantly or at all, and the search for the causes of sexual problems must move to emotional or psychological areas.

Finding Psychological Help

Most sexual problems have emotional components, even when the original cause is physical. Some are entirely emotional in origin. Much of what we have said about the competence and inclinations of medical doctors with regard to older people also holds true for psychotherapists and counselors. They tend to be unaware of and at times uninterested in the emotional problems of later life. They have usually had some training in sex education but rarely in the specialized area of sex after sixty. To find a therapist who can be of help to you will probably require determination.

There are several types of therapy to choose from. *Individual psychotherapy* means talking with a therapist one-to-one on a regular basis. *Marital counseling* involves both you and your partner. A broader term is *couples therapy,* which encompasses unmarried couples as well. *Family counseling* includes other members of your family. *Psychoanalysis* is an intensive form of individual psychotherapy, requiring several sessions a week. *Group psychotherapy* usually consists of a group of five to ten patients whose problems are discussed by the group under the guidance of one or two therapists. *Sex therapy* is a relatively new specialty, which concentrates on the actual sexual problem itself, teaching couples how to make love more effectively.

The background and training of therapists vary greatly. Psychotherapists can be *psychiatrists* (M.D.'s who specialize in psychiatry), *psychologists* (with master's or doctoral degrees in psychology) or *social workers* (with master's or doctoral degrees in social work). (The term "social worker" can be confusing, since people may define themselves as social workers because of the kind of work they do rather than because of their training. Ask if the social worker has, at minimum, a master's degree in social work.) *Psychoanalysts* have had advanced training in the psychoanalytic method. All these fields require a program of formal education and a supervised training period in psychotherapy or case work. All states require doctors to be licensed, and this is beginning to be true for practicing psychologists and social workers as well. Social workers who are certified (you will see the letters A.C.S.W.—for Academy of Certified Social Workers —after their names) by the National Association of Social Workers have had a period of professional training and examination beyond the master's degree.

In addition to psychotherapists, there are numerous other kinds of counselors. *Marriage counselors* work with marriage and sex problems. This is a still unregulated field and practitioners range from competent and well-trained professionals to quacks and charlatans. Be careful to investigate the credentials (professional training and experience) of anyone you are considering as a counselor. *Pastoral counseling* has grown out of the counseling role of the clergy, with individual clerics counseling, supervising, and training others to counsel. The quality of this counseling depends on the training and skills of each individual; there are no standard requirements for such training in theological schools.

Well-trained *sex therapists* are usually much more able than other health professionals to evaluate and help resolve specific sexual problems. A general rule is that if you are seeing your family doctor, cleric, etc., regarding sexual problems, resolution should begin to occur in six to eight sessions. If it doesn't, you should seek referral to a specialist in sex therapy. *All About Sex Therapy* by Peter R. Kilmen, M.D., and Katherine H. Mills, M.D. (Plenum Press, 1983) will help answer your questions about how sex therapy works.

Sex therapists have proliferated in recent years. Following Masters and Johnson's important clinical work in the treatment of sexual dysfunction, thousands of practitioners now offer such therapy. Many are untrained or poorly trained. Some are outright frauds. Because this is a new and unregulated field, without an organized structure of qualifications, requirements, examinations, clinical experience, or peer review—and because sexual problems are so susceptible to exploitation by skillful, smooth-talking incompetents—the choice of a sex counselor requires very careful consideration.

How do you find competent psychotherapists, counselors, and sex therapists? Some sources to check are university medical schools and clinical teaching hospitals (many have sex therapy clinics); local medical or psychiatric societies; university schools of social work; community mental health centers; senior centers; local chapters of the National Association of Social Workers, Inc. (write to 7981 Eastern Avenue, Silver Spring, MD 20910 for a listing of local chapters); the American Psychological Association (write to 1200 Seventeenth Street, N.W., Washington, DC 20036 for a list of psychological associations in your state); the National Association for Mental Health (write to 1021 Prince Street, Alexandria, VA 22314 for a list of local chapters); Family Service America (to find their member Family Service agencies write to 11700 West Lake Park Drive, Milwaukee, WI 53224); and your family doctor or cleric.

When talking to these suggested sources, be specific and ask for a therapist who will be interested in working with an older person in sex counseling. Ask for at least two names so you will be able to make a choice. Friends and acquaintances may be able to refer you to professionals who have been helpful to them, as long as you recognize that individual preferences vary considerably.

The National Institute of Mental Health's Center on Aging (9000 Rockville Pike, Bethesda, MD 20892) and the Gerontological Society's Social Research, Planning and Practice Section (1411 K Street, N.W., Suite 300, Washington, DC 20005) can be contacted for information. The American Association for Marriage and Family Therapy (924 West Ninth Street, Upland, CA 91786) is pressing for regulation of persons who call themselves marriage counselors and should be able to refer you to someone in your locale (including Canada). The American Association of Sex Educators, Counselors, and Therapists (11 Dupont Circle, N.W., Suite 220, Washington, DC 20036) certifies sex counselor–therapists and has a national roster from which names can be obtained. You may want to write the Masters and Johnson Institute (24 South Kingshighway, St. Louis, MO 63108) for referral to competent sex counselors near you who have been trained by them. The Sex Information and Education Council of the United States (SIECUS) (32 Washington Place, Room 52, New York University, New York, NY 10003) is an additional source of information and referral.

The cost of therapy varies from free clinics and free counseling, to sliding fees based on income, up to $125 or more for a fifty-minute session (in 1986). Group therapy is less costly than individual therapy. Some health insurance plans partially cover costs of psychotherapy. Many do not. Medicare allows only $250 a year for outpatient psychotherapy, and only if performed by a psychiatrist. Few insurance programs cover sex therapy per se. But Medicare pays for treatment of sexual dysfunction if the diagnosis can be included under the category of "psychophysiological genito-urinary disorder," diagnostic category 305.6 in the second edition of the American Psychiatric Association *Diagnostic and Statistical Manual of Mental Disorders* (DSM II). Recently some insurance companies have begun to request DSM III (third edition) diagnoses, which are more specific (for example, 302.71, 302.72). It is wise to inform your therapist of this fact, since it may not be widely known.

The amount of time required for evaluating and, if possible, resolving a particular sexual problem varies. Sometimes a single session can be enough. More often a series of weekly sessions is recommended, lasting from several months to more than a year or, in the case of psychoanalysis, a number of years.

What Happens in Psychotherapy?

You can't literally change the past, obviously, but you can gain perspective about it, change the way you feel about it, and break old habits and acquire new ways of coping effectively. Through talking about and exploring your past patterns, you may be helped to understand the sources of sexual problems, lose certain inhibitions, and learn new avenues of sexual expression. Therapeutic counseling does not simply dwell on the past, however. You will be discussing the here and now, your present relationships, always looking for your *own* responsibility for what is happening in your life. You will be asked questions, comments will be made (some may startle you), and suggestions may be proposed. Working out conflicts and going in new directions, therefore, come about through joint work by you *and* your therapist on the past and the present. You work together on your private life. The process may remind you of both parenting and teaching. You retain your basic personality, but hopefully you rid yourself of unwelcome symptoms, gain insight and enhanced well-being, and increase your effectiveness in everyday living. Altogether you are likely to feel better about yourself.

How should you act when you go to the therapist? Once again, be frank. Tell him or her whatever is troubling you. There are certain basic things you can require or expect:

▶ Your therapist needs to be well informed both about the problems of older people and about sexual problems. Don't be afraid to question therapists about their background, training, and general interest in these areas. Evaluate their answers (or failures to answer) in terms of what you now know—from this book and from your own experiences—to be important to you.

▶ The therapist should ask for your sexual, marital, and personal history, and probably will want a medical report from your doctor.

▶ You should feel a sense of rapport and comfort with the therapist by the time you have had several sessions. If not, talk over your feelings frankly. If matters do not improve, you may need to consider a different therapist, since rapport and trust are crucial to working effectively on sexual and emotional problems. Do not consider the need to change therapists the result of a flaw in yourself. Each individual's requirements in a relationship as close as that of therapist and patient will be different, and intangible but crucial factors like empathy, perception, manner, and attitude are involved in making the right choice. A personality and approach that are right for one person may be all wrong for another. As long as you are candid in your encounters with the therapist, you can trust your perceptions about whether he or she is a good choice for you.

As for your part in therapy, you must learn to:

▶ Set aside shyness and embarrassment.
▶ Open your mind and feelings to new ideas and insights.
▶ Be willing to actively try new directions in your relationships with others.
▶ Realize that while many things can improve, some things cannot. Once you have decided which is which, with the aid of the therapist, you can begin to take advantage of those areas where improvement can realistically occur.

What Happens in Sex Therapy?

Sex therapy is a unique, usually short-term form of therapy that has evolved over the past twenty years under the leadership of Dr. William Masters and Virginia Johnson of St. Louis. This method is particularly effective for the rapid treatment of problems like premature ejaculation, vaginal spasm, failure to achieve orgasm, and some forms of impotence. It is more difficult, but not impossible, to treat low or absent sexual desire or lack of pleasure in sex. The original Masters and Johnson techniques required a male and female therapist for each couple, a two-week stay in a hotel near the treatment center (so the couple was isolated and could concentrate on therapy), and daily therapy sessions. Patients were given two years of follow-up assistance from therapists available twenty-four hours a day, usually by telephone, for no extra charge. Most sex therapists have now modified this so that couples can remain in their own communities and homes and have therapy once or twice a week for about fourteen sessions. Educational counseling about sex, improving communication between a couple, and carrying out "pleasuring exercises" are all part of treatment. Therapists may use movies and slides in their teaching, as well as group therapy. Couples with marital problems that go beyond their sexual difficulties are encouraged to obtain marital counseling and/or individual psychotherapy. Individuals who are not part of a couple are also accepted for sex therapy.

Even sexual problems that have existed for many years have the possibility of resolution. This is true whether your sexual problems are new or long-term. As long as they are troubling to you, you owe it to yourself to see what can be done to resolve them. In many cases you will be rewarded with good results.

Chapter 11

The Second Language of Sex

C an sex really remain interesting and exciting after forty, fifty, or sixty years of adulthood? Older people themselves have testified that it can. Affection, warmth, and sensuality do not have to deteriorate with age and may, in fact, increase.

Sex in later life is sex for its own sake: pleasure, release, communication, shared intimacy. Except for older men involved with younger women, it is no longer associated with childbearing and the creation of families. This freedom can be both exhilarating and insightful, especially for those who have literally never had the time until now to think about and get to know themselves and each other.

Love and sex can mean many different things to older people. Some of them will be obvious to you; others less so:

▶ *The opportunity for expression of passion, affection, admiration, loyalty, and other positive emotions.* This can occur in longterm relationships that have steadily grown and developed over the years, in relationships that actually improve in later years, and in new relationships such as second or third marriages.

▶ *An affirmation of one's body and its functioning.* Active sex demonstrates to older people that their bodies are still capable of working well and providing pleasure. For many people, satisfactory sexual functioning is an extremely important part of their lives and helps to maintain high morale and enthusiasm.

▶ *A strong sense of self.* Sexuality is one of the ways people get a sense of their identity—who they are and what their impact is on others. Positive reactions from others preserve and enhance self-esteem. Feeling "feminine" or "masculine," whatever meaning these terms have for each individual, is connected with feeling valued as a person. Negative reactions depress and discourage older people and may tempt them to write off their sexuality forever.

▶ *A means of self-assertion.* The patterns of self-assertion available when people are young change as they grow older. Their children are grown-up and gone; their jobs are usually behind them; personal and social relationships now become far more important as outlets for expressing personality. Sex can be a valuable means of positive self-assertion. One man told us, "I feel like a million dollars when I make love even though we are scrimping along on Social Security. My wife has always made me feel like a great success in bed and I believe I do the same for her. We've been able to stand a lot of stress in life because of our closeness this way."

▶ *Protection from anxiety.* The intimacy and the closeness of sexual union bring security and significance to people's lives, particularly when the outside world threatens them with hazards and losses. An older couple we know described the warmth of their sexual life as "a port in the storm," a place to escape from worry and trouble. A very much older woman, concerned with eventual death, called sex "the ultimate closeness against the night." Sex serves as an important means of feeling in charge when other elements of one's life feel out of control.

▶ *Defiance of the stereotypes of aging.* Familiar though they are with the derogatory attitudes of society toward late-life sex, older people who are sexually active defy the neutered status expected of them. We have had them say to us, "We're not finished yet," "I'm not ready to kick the bucket," "You can't keep a good man [woman] down," or "There may be snow on the roof but there's still fire in the furnace."

▶ *The pleasure of being touched or caressed.* Older widows, widowers, and divorced people describe how much they miss the simple pleasure and warmth of physical closeness, of being touched, held, and caressed by someone they care for. Holding and hugging friends, children, and pets offers some compensation but does not replace the special intimacy and feeling of being cared about that can exist in a good relationship or sexual union.

▶ *A sense of romance.* The courting aspects of sexuality may be highly significant—flowers, soft lights, music, a sense of romantic pursuit, elegance, sentiment, and courtliness—and give pleasure in themselves. Romance may continue even when sexual intercourse, for various reasons, ceases. Mr. and Mrs. Denham, a couple in their eighties, described their evenings together to us. They typically bathe and dress for dinner, she in a long dress, he in a suit and tie. They dine with candlelight and music, listen to music during the evening, hold hands, and enjoy each other's companionship. At bedtime they fall asleep in each other's arms. Often they awaken in the middle of the night and have long, intimate conversations, sleeping late the next morning. Mr. Denham said of his wife, "I fall in love with her every day. My feelings grow stronger when I realize we have only a certain amount of time left."

▶ *An affirmation of life.* Sex expresses joy and continued affirmation of life. The quality of one's most intimate relationships is an important measure of whether life has been worthwhile. Otherwise successful people may count their lives a failure if they have been unable to achieve significant closeness to other people, never felt fully desired or accepted. Conversely, people with modest accomplishments may feel highly satisfied about themselves if they have been affirmed through intimate relationships. Sexual intimacy is only one way of achieving intimacy, of course, but it is an especially profound affirmation of the worthwhileness of life.

▶ *A continuing search for sensual growth and experience.* Some older people continue to search throughout their lives for ways to create new excitement and experiences. Some who are dissatisfied with their present lives look for ways to improve them. Others seek marriage counseling, pursue divorce, remarriage, or new relationships in the hope of finding what they are searching for. Many can find this growth and excitement within their present relationship if they learn some of the skills that make it possible. Love and sex are twin arts requiring effort and knowledge. Only in fairy tales do people live happily ever after without working at it. It takes a continuous and active effort to master the processes that eradicate emotional distances between yourself and another and to continue to grow and learn.

When people are young and first getting used to sexuality, their sex tends to be urgent and explosive, involved largely with physical pleasure and in many cases the conception of children. This is the *first language of sex*. It is biological and instinctive, with wonderfully exciting and energizing potentialities. The process of discovering one's ability to be sexually desirable and sexually effective often becomes a way of asserting independence, strength, prowess, and power. The first language of sex has been much discussed and written about because it is easy to study and measure—one can tabulate physical response, frequency of contacts, forms of outlet, sexual positions, and physical skills in lovemaking. But sex is not just a matter of athletics and "production." Some people recognize this early on and simultaneously develop a *second language of sex,* which is emotional and communicative as well as physical. Others continue largely in the first language—sometimes all their lives, sometimes only until they begin to see its limitations and desire something more.

The second language is largely learned rather than instinctive and is often vastly underdeveloped since it depends upon the ability to recognize and share feelings in words, actions, and unspoken perceptions, and to achieve mutual tenderness and thoughtfulness with another person. In its richest form, the second language becomes highly creative and imaginative, with bountiful possibilities for new emotional experiences. Yet it is a slow-developing art, acquired deliberately and painstakingly through years of experience in giving and receiving.

In the natural flow of events in the life cycle, times will come when you may find yourself re-evaluating many areas of your life, including your sexuality. Middle age is the time when people typically begin to take stock of their lives and reassess their work, their personal relationships, their social and spiritual commitments. Retirement is another time when re-evaluations take place. Both periods can be chaotic, generating emotional upsets, divorce, higher risk of alcoholism, and other evidences of stress.

But these can be constructive as well as dangerous ages, and the second language of sex has a good deal to offer you if you want to move in new directions in your personal life. Shared tenderness, warmth, humor, merriment, anger, passion, sorrow, camaraderie, fear—feelings of every conceivable sort can flow back and forth in a sexual relationship that has matured to this level of development.

Part of the secret of learning the second language lies in learning how to give. Receiving is much easier. It makes few demands. But the habit of only taking deadens the impulse to reciprocate. As Erich Fromm wrote in *The Art of Loving* (1956), "Most people see the problem of love primarily as that of being loved, rather than that of loving, of one's capacity to love." Giving is *not* an endless gift of yourself to others in which you expect nothing in return. Nor is it a marketplace transaction, trading with the expectation of an equal exchange. Healthy giving involves not only the hopeful and human anticipation that something equally good will be returned but also the pleasures inherent in giving, regardless of return. The balance to be struck must be chosen by each person and worked out in partnership.

The second language implies sensitivity. It means clearing up long-held grudges and old irritations toward your partner and people in general so your energy is not wasted in negativity. It suggests the possibility of renewing love every day. It requires knowing what pleases your partner and what pleases you. It involves playfulness as well as passion, and talking, laughing, teasing, sharing secrets, reminiscing, telling jokes, making plans, confessing fears and uncertainties, crying—in the privacy of shared companionship. It need not involve the sex act at all.

If boredom creeps into the relationship, both partners need to acknowledge it; it is time to look for or listen to the deeper feelings that each of you has hidden away against the time when the richness of such feelings will be welcome and restorative. You have to resist the pulls of habit. Routines and responsibilities may have dulled the impulse to really talk, and you must fight against succumbing to the temptation to withdraw into your own self-absorbed world. Self-centeredness, wanting sexual and emotional contact only when you are in the mood, without concern for your partner's needs, is guaranteed to produce conflict. Competitiveness based on some fancied level of sexual performance is also deadly.

The second language of sex can be developed by actively trying to learn it. Older people may have struggled throughout their lives to overcome obstacles, earn a living, raise a family, and carry out other responsibilities. In doing so they have literally sacrificed their private lives and individual growth to this process. But fortunately love and sex are *always* there to be rediscovered, enhanced, or even appreciated for the very first time, whether you are young or very old. Self-starters have the advantage over those who wait passively for love to strike like lightning.

Older people have, in fact, a special ability to bring love and sex to new levels of development because they are more experienced. Many people do learn from experience. They develop perceptions that are connected with the unique sense of having lived a long time and having struggled to come to terms with life as a cycle from birth to death. A number of these qualities are beautifully suited to the flourishing of the second language. An appreciation of the preciousness of life and the valuing of immediateness can occur as people become older. What counts now is the present moment, where once it was the casually expected future. If the developing awareness of the brevity of life leads you to come to terms with your own mortality in a mature and healthy way, no longer denying it, you will find you no longer live heedlessly, as though you had all the time in the world. The challenge of living as richly as possible in the time you have left is exhilarating, not depressing.

Elementality—the enjoyment of the elemental things of life— may develop in late life precisely because older people are more keenly aware that life is short. Such people may find themselves becoming more adept in separating out the important from the trivial. Responsiveness to nature, human warmth, children, music, beauty in any form, may be heightened. Healthy late life is frequently a time for greater enjoyment of all the senses— colors, sights, sounds, smells, touch—and less involvement with the transient drives for achievement, possessions, and power.

Older people have time for love. Although they have fewer years left to live than the young and middle-aged, they can often spend more time on social and sexual relationships than any other age group if they are in reasonably good health. It is true that many have limited financial resources, but fortunately social and personal relationships are among the pleasures in life that can be free of charge.

Willingness to change counts, as well. It is possible to become quite different in later life from what you were in youth. Obviously, the change can go in positive or negative directions. But the point to remember is that change is possible. You do not need to become locked into any particular mode of behavior at any time of life. Experimentation and learning are possible all along the life cycle, and this holds true for sex and love. Naturally, the more actively you grow, the greater the reservoir of experience and the larger the repertoire you can draw upon in getting along with and loving other people.

The early and middle years set the stage, but perhaps only in the later years can life with its various choices and possibilities have the chance to shape itself into something approximating a human work of art. And perhaps only in later life, when personality reaches its final stages of development, can lovemaking and sex achieve the fullest possible growth. Sex does not merely exist in the later years; it holds the possibility of becoming greater than it ever was.

The special psychology of sex in the second half of life will eventually be better understood than it is now. Then we will comprehend for the first time the full life cycle of love and sexuality—with youth a time for exciting exploration and self-discovery; middle age, for gaining skill, confidence, and discrimination; and old age, for bringing the experience of a lifetime and the unique perspectives of the final years of life to the art of loving one another. We have a great deal yet to learn from those who personally have mastered this complex and wonderful art over years of time.

Glossary

Androgen Any of the *steroid** hormones produced by the adrenal glands and the *testes* that develop and maintain masculine characteristics; *testosterone* is the best known.

Anus The opening from the lower bowel (colon) through which solid waste is passed.

Atrophy A wasting away or diminution in size of a cell, tissue, organ, part, or body.

Bartholin's glands Two small, roundish bodies, one on each side of the vaginal opening. Although they produce mucus in sexual excitement, they are not the primary source of vaginal lubrication during intercourse.

Benign prostatic hypertrophy (BPH) Noncancerous enlargement of the *prostate* gland that occurs in the middle and later years.

Bladder The distendable elastic sac that serves as a receptacle and place of storage for the urine.

Cervix The part of the *uterus,* sometimes called the neck, which protrudes into the *vagina.*

Circumcision Surgical removal of the foreskin, a loose fold of skin that surrounds the head of the *penis.*

Climacteric See **Menopause.**

Climax See **Orgasm.**

* Words italicized are defined elsewhere in the Glossary.

Clitoris   A small, erectile organ at the upper end of the *vulva,* homologous with the *penis,* and a significant focus of sexual excitement and *orgasm* in the woman.

Coitus   Copulation, coition, sexual intercourse.

Cowper's glands   A pair of small glands lying alongside and discharging into the male *urethra.* They contribute lubrication during sexual activity.

Cystitis   Inflammation of the urinary bladder.

Dyspareunia   The occurrence of pain in the sexual act, usually experienced in the female vaginal area.

Ejaculation   The forceful emission of the seminal fluid at *orgasm.*

Ejaculatory impotence   Inability to ejaculate.

Erogenous zones   Sensitive areas of the body, such as the mouth, lips, buttocks, breasts, and genital areas, which are important in sexual arousal.

Estrogen   One of the active female hormones produced by the *ovaries* and the adrenal glands, which has a profound effect on the generative organs and breasts.

Fallopian tube   The tube that leads from each *ovary* into the *uterus;* after *ovulation* the ovum travels through the tube on its way to the *uterus* and fertilization takes place in the tube.

Flashes (or **flushes**), **hot**   A symptom associated with the hormonal changes during *menopause,* caused by a sudden rapid dilation of blood vessels.

Foreplay   Sexual acts which precede intercourse during which the partners stimulate each other by kissing, touching, and caressing.

Frigidity   An imprecise term applied to various aspects of female sexual inadequacy: (1) popularly, abnormal lack of desire, or coldness; (2) inability to achieve an *orgasm* through intercourse; (3) inability to achieve orgasm by any means; (4) any other level of sexual response considered unsatisfactory by the woman or her partner.

Genital area   The area which contains the external genital organs such as the *vulva* in the female and the *penis* in the male.

Genitalia The reproductive organs, especially the external organs.

Hormones Chemical substances produced in the ductless (endocrine) glands of the body and discharged directly into the bloodstream. They have specific effects upon the activity of a certain organ or organs. Sexual hormones regulate the entire reproductive cycle. (The body produces many nonsexual hormones as well.)

Hormone therapy The medical use of supplementary hormones (other than or in addition to those produced by the endocrine glands) for treatment of diseases and deficiencies.

Impotence Lack of erectile power in the male *penis,* which prevents copulation.

Labia Two rounded folds of tissue that form the outer boundaries of the external genitals in the female.

Libido Sexual desire.

Mastectomy Surgical removal of a breast.

Masturbation Stimulation of the sex organs, usually to *orgasm,* through manual or mechanical means.

Medical specialties regarding sex:

> **Endocrinology** The functions and diseases of the ductless (endocrine) glands.

> **Gynecology** The diseases, reproductive functions, organs, and endocrinology of females.

> **Urology** The functions, organs, and diseases of the urinary system in males and females and of the reproductive system in males.

Menopause The time of life for the human female, usually between the ages of 45 and 55, which is marked by the cessation of *menstruation* and *ovulation.* It may be gradual or sudden, and it can last from three months to three years, or even longer. It marks the end of the childbearing potential.

Menstruation The periodic discharge of the body fluid (menses) from the *uterus* through the vagina, occurring normally once a month.

Nocturnal emission   Ejaculation of *semen* at night while asleep; often called a wet dream.

Oral-genital sex   Forms of stimulation of the genitalia by the mouth:

Cunnilingus   Stimulation of vulva (especially the clitoris and labia) by the partner's mouth and tongue.

Fellatio   Stimulation of the penis by the partner's mouth and tongue.

Orchidectomy (orchiectomy)   Removal of one or both *testes;* castration.

Orgasm   The culmination of the sex act. There is a feeling of sudden, intense pleasure accompanied by an abrupt increase in pulse rate and blood pressure. Involuntary spasms of pelvic muscles cause relief of sexual tension with vaginal contractions in the female and *ejaculation* by the male. It lasts up to ten seconds.

Ovaries   The two major reproductive glands of the female, in which the ova (eggs) are formed and *estrogen,* or female hormones, are produced.

Ovulation   The process in which a mature egg is discharged by an *ovary* for possible fertilization.

Papanicolaou smear (Pap smear) test   A simple test to determine the presence of cancer of the *uterus* by analyzing cells taken from the *cervix* or *vagina.*

Penis   The male organ of sexual intercourse.

Perineum   (1) The internal portion of the body in the pelvis occupied by urogenital passages and the rectum; (2) the internal and external region between the *scrotum* and *anus* in the man, and the *vulva* and *anus* in the woman.

Pituitary gland   An endocrine gland consisting of three lobes, located at the base of the brain. The body's "master gland," it controls the other endocrine glands and influences growth, metabolism and maturation.

Potency   Sexual capacity for intercourse; the ability to achieve and sustain erection. Applied only to the male.

Premature ejaculation   Almost instant *ejaculation* (within 3 seconds) upon entry of the *penis* into the *vagina*.

Prostate   A walnut-sized body, partly muscular and partly glandular, which surrounds the base of the urethra in the male. It secretes a milky fluid which is discharged into the *urethra* at the time of emission of *semen*.

Prostatectomy   Surgical removal of part or all of the *prostate*. There are three types, depending upon the anatomical approach: (1) transurethral (TUR); (2) suprapubic (or retropubic); and (3) perineal.

Prostatism, prostatitis   Inflammation or congestion in the *prostate*.

Refractory period   See **Sexual response cycle.**

Replacement therapy   See **Hormone therapy.**

Scrotum   The sac containing the *testes*.

Semen   The whitish fluid containing sperm, which is discharged in *ejaculation*.

Sensuality   The wider aspect of *sexuality;* the involvement of all the physical senses that enhance and express one's sexuality.

Sex   (1) Urge for and (2) act of sexual union.

Sex hormones   See **Hormones.** Sexual hormones regulate the entire reproductive cycle.

Sexual dysfunction   A general term for different varieties and degrees of unsatisfying sexual response and performance.

Sexual fantasies   Vivid and excitatory imaginings about sex; healthy and common in both sexes.

Sexual response cycle   The physical changes that occur in the body during sexual excitement and orgasm. It includes four phases: (1) the excitement or erotic-arousal phase during foreplay; (2) the intromission or plateau phase; (3) the orgasmic or climax phase; and (4) the resolution or recovery phase. The time required for the completion of recovery—the time required before the first phase can be successfully initiated again—is called the refractory period. The refractory period is more critical to the male.

Sexuality The emotional and physical responsiveness to sexual stimuli. Also, one's sexual identity, role and perception; one's femininity; one's masculinity.

Sperm Spermatozoa, the male reproductive cells, produced by the *testes* and discharged during intercourse into the *vagina.*

Sterility The incapacity to reproduce sexually; infertility.

Steroids A class of chemical substances that includes the *sex hormones.*

Testes (testicles) The two male reproductive glands, located in the cavity of the *scrotum,* the source of spermatozoa and the androgens.

Testosterone A male hormone (an *androgen*), a *steroid,* produced by the testes.

Thyroid gland The gland partially surrounding the windpipe (trachea) in the neck whose function is to supply hormones which adjust the metabolism of the body.

Urethra The passage or canal in the *penis* through which the male discharges both urine and *sperm.* In women the passage through which urine passes.

Urethritis Inflammation of the *urethra.*

Urogenital system The organs that serve the functions of urination, sexual activity, and procreation.

Uterus (womb) The hollow muscular organ in the female in which the embryo and fetus develop to maturity.

Vagina The tube or sheath leading from the *uterus* to the *vulva* at the exterior of the body. It receives the *penis* during intercourse.

Vaginitis Inflammation of the *vagina.*

Vas deferens The duct from each *testicle* that carries *sperm* to the *penis.*

Venereal disease Any disease which is transmitted during sexual intercourse.

Virility Masculine vigor, including potency (from which it must be distinguished), sexual prowess (skill), sexual frequency, and attractiveness.

Vulva   The external female genitalia, including the *labia, clitoris,* and the outer *vagina.*

Womb   See **Uterus.**

Bibliography

Almvig, Chris. *The Invisible Minority: Aging and Lesbianism.* Utica, NY: Department of Gerontology, University of Syracuse at Utica, 1982.

Berger, Raymond M. *Gay and Gray: The Older Homosexual Man.* Champaign, IL: University of Illinois Press, 1982.

Brecher, Edward M., and the Editors of Consumer Reports Books. *Love, Sex and Aging.* Boston: Little, Brown, 1984.

Comfort, Alex. *The Joy of Sex.* New York: Crown, 1972.

———, ed. *Sexual Consequences of Disability.* Philadelphia: Stickley, 1978.

Fromm, Erich. *The Art of Loving.* New York: Harper & Row, 1956.

Gay, Peter. *The Bourgeois Experience: Victoria to Freud.* Vol. 1, *Education of the Senses.* New York: Oxford University Press, 1984.

Hite, Shere. *The Hite Report: A Nationwide Study on Female Sexuality.* New York: Dell, 1976.

Kaplan, Helen S. *The Evaluation of Sexual Disorder: Psychological and Medical Aspects.* New York: Bruner/Mazel, 1983.

Kinsey, Alfred C., Wardell Pomeroy, and Clyde E. Martin. *Sexual Behavior in the Human Male.* Philadelphia: W.B. Saunders, 1948.

Kinsey, Alfred C., Wardell Pomeroy, Clyde E. Martin, and Paul

Bibliography

M. Gebhard. *Sexual Behavior in the Human Female.* Philadelphia: W.B. Saunders, 1955.

Masters, William H., and Virginia E. Johnson. *Human Sexual Response.* Boston: Little, Brown, 1966.

————. *Human Sexual Inadequacy.* Boston: Little, Brown, 1970.

Rothman, Ellen. *Hands and Hearts: A History of Courtship in America.* New York: Basic Books, 1984.

Sherfey, Mary J. *The Nature and Evolution of Female Sexuality.* New York: World, 1973.

Starr, Bernard D., and Marcella B. Weiner. *The Starr-Weiner Report on Sex and Sexuality in the Mature Years.* Briarcliff Manor, NY: Stein and Day, 1981.

Weg, Ruth B., ed. *Sexuality in the Later Years.* Orlando, FL: Academic Press, 1983.

The only medical journal that covers clinical and psychosocial components of sexuality and family life is *Medical Aspects of Sexuality,* 500 Plaza Drive, Secaucus, NJ 07094. It is published monthly.

Index

AARP (American Association of Retired Persons), 120–21
Abdomen, protruding, 85
Abstinence, self-imposed, 7
Acne, 61
Acquired immune deficiency syndrome (AIDS), 53–57
ACTH (adrenocorticotropic hormone), 62
Activities, social, 118, 119
Acyclovir (Zovirax), 58
Adrenocorticosteroids (prednisone, etc.), 62
Adrenocorticotropic hormone (ACTH), 62
Advice, financial, 143–44
Aerobic exercise, 82–83, 88
Aesthetic narrowness, 5
Affairs, 129–30
Age:
    and erection problems, 45
    and estrogen replacement, 16
    and sexual desire, 3
Ageism, 4
Aging process, 28
    emotional problems, 98
AIDS, 53–57
Air pollution, 95

Alcohol, 52, 65–66, 68
    and bladder infections, 22
    and chronic prostatitis, 36
    and hypertension, 34
    and osteoporosis, 19, 90
    for relaxation, 133
Aldactone (spironolactone), 61, 62, 63
Aldomet (methyldopa), 61, 62, 63, 64
All About Sex Therapy, Kilmen and Mills, 153
Allergies, 11
    and estrogen replacement, 13
Ambilhar (niridazole), 62
American Association of Retired Persons (AARP), 120–21
Amphetamines, 61, 67
Anabolic drugs, 61
Analgesics, 64
Anal intercourse, 55
Androgens, 8, 61, 62, 63
Anemia, 39–40, 90
Anger, chronic illness and, 110
Angina pectoris, 32
Antabuse (disulfiram), 61, 62
Antacids, and osteoporosis, 19
Antiarrhythmic drugs, 34

Antibiotics:
  for sexually transmitted diseases,
    58, 59
  to prevent urinary tract infection,
    22
Anticholinergics, 61
Anticipatory grief, 113
Antidepressants, 60–64, 66
Antihistamines, 62, 66
Antihypertensives, 47, 60–63, 64
Antimalarials, 62
Anxiety:
  protection from, 160
  short-term medication, 34
Aphrodisiacs, alleged, 51–52
Appetite loss, 40
Arousal, 105
  and heart problems, 31–32
  impaired, 61
Arrhythmias, 34
Arteriosclerosis, 47, 50
Arthritis, 37–39, 90
The Art of Loving, Fromm, 163
Aspirin, 37, 62
Assertion of self, 160
Asthma, and estrogen replacement
  therapy, 13
Athletic standards of sexual
  performance, 5
Atromid-S (clofibrate), 61, 62
Atrophic vaginitis, 10, 12, 13, 16,
  20
  and estrogen replacement, 14
Attitudes to sex, 2–5, 100–101,
  103
Aureomycin (chlortetracycline), 63
Azulfidine (sulfasalazine), 62

Backache, 39
Back muscles, exercise for, 85
Baclofen (Lioresal), 61, 62

Bactrim (co-trimoxazole), 62
Banthine (methantheline), 62
Barbiturates, 61, 62, 67
Basketball, 83
BCNU, 63
Beauty, physical, ideas of, 5
Beds, 131–32
Benign prostatic hyperplasia (BPH),
  74–78
Beta blockers, 34, 47
Bilateral salpingo-ovariectomy, 69
Biofeedback training, and stress
  incontinence, 41
Biopsy, endometrial, and estrogen
  replacement therapy, 20
Bladder, irritation in intercourse, 11
Blisters, in genital area, 57
Blood clotting problems, and
  estrogen replacement, 20
Blood pressure, during sex, 30
Blood tests, and estrogen therapy,
  20
Body, affirmation of, 159
*Bonnie Prudden's After Fifty Fitness
  Guide,* 85
Boredom with sex, 107, 164
BPH (benign prostatic hyperplasia),
  74–78
Brain disease, 49
Bran cereal, 89
Breast problems:
  cancer, 70–73
  enlargement, 61
    male, 16, 63
  and estrogen replacement, 13,
    17–18
Bronchitis, 43
Bulk, in diet, 89
Burtoff v. *Burtoff,* 147
Bus travel, 121
Busulfan (Myleran), 63
Butyl nitrate, 67

Caffeine, 22, 90, 93
Calcium, dietary, 90–91
  increased urinary excretion, 19
Calcium blockers, 34
Calisthenics, 83
Calorie requirements, 91–92
Cancer, 69
  of breast, 70–73
  and estrogen therapy, 14, 20
  and genital herpes, 57
  of prostate, 75–77
  rectal, 80
Cantharidin, 52
Capsicum, 52
Carbohydrates, 87
Carbonated beverages, 19
Cardiac pacemakers, 33
Casale, Anne, *The Long Life Cookbook,* 88
Casual sex, 55
Catapres (clonidine), 61, 62, 63
Cellulite, 90
Cerebrovascular accident, 35
Cervix, cancer of, 69
  and genital herpes, 57
Change, 165
  physical, of age, 8–28
Change of life. *See* Menopause
Child molestation, 3
Children, 6
  living with, 128–29
  problems with, 140–47
Chinese ginseng, 52
Chlamydia, 37, 50
Chlorambucil (Leukeran), 62
Chlordiazepoxide (Librium), 61, 62, 63
Chlormadinone, 63
Chlorpromazine (Thorazine), 61, 62, 63
Chlortetracycline (Aureomycin), 63
Cholesterol, 34, 88–89

Chronic illness, 110–11
  cystitis, 40
  emphysema, 43
  prostatitis, 36–37
  renal disease, 42
Cigarette smoking. *See* Smoking
Cimetidine (Tagamet), 61, 62, 63, 65
Cimicifugin, 52
Cities, social activities, 119
Classified ads, 122
Clifford, Denis, *Legal Guide for Lesbian and Gay Couples,* 115
Climacteric. *See* Menopause
Clitoris:
  changes in, 11, 61
  stimulation of, 134–35
Clofibrate (Atromid-S), 61, 62
Clonidine (Catapres), 19, 61, 62, 63
Cocaine, 62, 63, 66–67
Colchicine, 62
Colostomy, 79–80
Communal living, 120
Communication with partner, 138–39
Community centers, 119
Companionship, personal qualities, 123
Competitiveness, 164
Computer dating services, 122
Condoms, 55
Congestive heart failure, 33
Conjugated estrogens, 14, 20, 63
Constipation, 89–90
Contraindications to estrogen replacement, 13, 15
Coping with Hysterectomy, Morgan, 70
Coronary bypass surgery, 33–34
Coronary dilators, 32
Corticosteroids, 37, 64

Cortisone, for Peyronie's disease, 42

Cortisone-related drugs, 19

Cost of sex therapy, 155

Co-trimoxazole (Bactrim, Septra), 62

Cotton panties, 21

Couples therapy, 152

Cranberry juice, 22

Cross-country skiing, 83

Cryosurgery, 77

Cubeb, 52

Curry, Hayden, *Legal Guide for Lesbian and Gay Couples,* 115

Cycling, 83

Cyclophosphamide (Cytoxan), 62

Cystitis, 10–11, 21, 22, 40

Cystocele, 41

Cytoxan (cyclophosphamide), 62

Damiana, 52

Dance, 83, 122

Dating services, 122

Deafness, 94–95

Death, during intercourse, 32

Debenzyline (phenoxybenzamine), 62

Deep vein thrombophlebitis, and estrogen replacement, 14, 15

Delestrogen (estradiol valerate), 20

Dependency of children, 140–41

Depo-Estradiol (estradiol cypionate), 20

Depression, 34
  with cystitis, 40
  after mastectomy, 71
  Parkinson's disease and, 41
  and penile prostheses, 49

Dermabrasion, 97

DES (diethylstilbestrol), 63

Desyrel (trazodone), 67

DeVries, Herbert, *Fitness After Forty: An Exercise Prescription for Lifelong Health,* 85

Diabetes, 35–36, 47, 90
  and estrogen replacement, 13, 15
  and exercise, 84
  fungus infections, 11

Diagnosis of impotence causes, 46–47

Diazepam (Valium), 61, 62

Diet, 48, 86–92
  and osteoporosis, 19, 90–91
  and prostate problems, 74
  and skin, 95
  and urinary tract infections, 22–23

Diethylstilbestrol (DES), 63

Digestive disorders, and calcium intake, 91

Digitalis, 62, 63

Digoxin (Lanoxin), 62

Discharge, vaginal, 11

Disease, 27–28
  prevention, by diet, 88
  and sexuality, 29–59, 150

Disinterest in sex, 6–7

Disopyramide (Norpace), 62

Disulfiram (Antabuse), 61, 62

Diuretics, 62, 64

Divorce, 108–9
  premarital agreements and, 146–47

Divorced women, views of, 125

Doctors, questions from, 150–51

Dosage of estrogens, 15–16, 17, 19

Double beds, 131–32

Douching, 11, 21, 136

Drugs:
  and AIDS, 54
  sexual effects, 60–68

Dryness of vagina, 9–10
Dynamic fitness, 82
Dyspareunia, 10, 40

Early old age, 4
Edecrin (ethacrynic acid), 62
Ejaculation, 24–26, 62
Electric blankets, 95
Electrocardiograms, 31
Elementality, 165
Embolism, and estrogen, 13
Emotional problems, 9, 98–115, 152
    after hysterectomy, 69–70
Emphysema, chronic, 43
Endocrine disorders, 47
Endometrial cancer, 16, 20
Endometriosis, 10
    and estrogen replacement, 13
Endorphins, 39
Enshrinement, 113–14, 141
Epilepsy, and estrogen, 13
Equilid (sulpiride), 61
Erections, 24, 44–45
    impaired, drug effects, 62, 64
    stimulation for, 135
    See also Impotence
Ergot, 19, 52
Escort services, 123
The Essential Guide to Prescription Drugs, Long, 67
Esterified estrogens (Evex, Menest), 20
Estrace (micronized 17-B estradiol), 20
Estraderm-50, 20
Estradiol cypionate (Depo-Estradiol), 20
Estradiol valerate (Delestrogen), 20
Estriol (Hormonin), 20

Estrogen, 8, 9, 41, 61, 62, 63
    replacement therapy, 10, 13–21, 91
    and sexual activity, 12
Ethacrynic acid (Edecrin), 62
Ethionamide (Trecator-SC), 62, 63
Evex (esterified estrogen), 20
Excitement, search for, 161–62
Exercise, 82–86
    for arthritis, 37–38
    and backache, 39
    after coronary bypass surgery, 33, 34
    and heart problems, 30–31
    and hypertension, 34
    and osteoporosis, 19, 90
Exploitation, 124–25
Expression of emotions, 159
Extramarital relations, death during intercourse, 32

Fallopian tubes, water in, 10
False aphrodisiacs, 51–52
Family counseling, 152
Family pictures, 132
Fantasies, sexual, 138–39
Fast action sports, 83
Fatal illness, 111
Fatigue, 9, 40
Fats, 87
Fear of impotence, 98–100
Female hormones, 8, 9
Femininity, and estrogen, 15
Feminization, 63
Fenfluramine (Pondimin), 61, 62
Fertility, male, 26, 62
Fibrocystic breast changes, and estrogen replacement, 13
Fibroid tumors of uterus, 69
    and estrogen replacement, 13, 14, 15

Fibrous cavernitis. *See* Peyronie's disease
Fish, fatty, 89
Fitness After Forty: An Exercise Prescription for Lifelong Health, DeVries and Hales, 85
Fluids, 22
  retention, and estrogen, 14
Folk figures, idealized, 2
Folk remedies for impotence, 51–52
Food and Drug Administration (FDA), and aphrodisiacs, 51–52
Freezing, for prostate cancer, 77
Friedman, E. H., 31
Frigidity, 104, 134
Fromm, Erich, *The Art of Loving,* 163
Fulvicin (griseofulvin), 63
Fungus infections, 11
Furadantin (nitrofurantoin), 62
Furosemide (Lasix), 62

Gadgets, 136
Gallbladder disease, 90
  and estrogen replacement, 13, 14, 15, 20
Genisis (conjugated estrogen), 20
Genital herpes, 57–58
  and AIDS, 55
Genitals, female, washing of, 22
Geriatrics, specialists in, 149
Ginseng, 51–52
Girdles, 21
Giving, 163
Galactorrhea, 61
Goldstein, Irwin, 48
Gonder, Maurice, 77
Gonorrhea, 58
Gout, 90

Gray Panthers, 121
Greenburger, Monroe, *What Every Man Should Know About His Prostate,* 74
Grief, 112–14
Grievances of children, 142
Griseofulvin (Fulvicin), 63
Group psychotherapy, 152
Guanethidine (Ismelin), 62, 64
Guilt feelings, 6, 102–4
Gynecomastia, 63

Habit, 131
Haldol (haloperidol), 61, 62, 63
Hales, Diane, *Fitness After Forty: An Exercise Prescription for Lifelong Health,* 85
Haloperidol (Haldol), 61, 62, 63
Halsted radical mastectomy, 73
Handball, 83
Headache, 9, 40
Health, and sexual interest, 7
Health clubs, 84
Health insurance, and psychotherapy, 155
Hearing problems, 94–95
Heart attack, 29–30
  and estrogen replacement, 13
  and exercise, 84
Heart disease, 29–34
  and estrogen replacement, 13
Heat treatments, 38
Hellerstein, H. E., 31
Hellerstein's Sexercise Tolerance Test, 31
Heparin, 63
Hernia, 41, 43
Heroin, 61, 62, 63, 66
Herpes simplex 2 virus, 57
HERS (Hysterectomy Educational Resources and Services), 69

High blood pressure, 34–35
 and calcium intake, 91
 and estrogen replacement, 13, 14
High-density-lipoprotein (HDL)
 cholesterol, 88
HIP (Help for Incontinent People),
 41
Hip discomfort, 37–38
Hirsutism, 61
Home remedies for women, 17, 21–
 23
Homosexual relationships, 114–15,
 116
Honeymoon cystitis, 11, 23
Hormones, 8–9, 27, 47–48
 replacement therapy, 13–21
Hormonin (estriol), 20
Hot flashes, 9, 17–19
 and estrogen replacement, 14, 15
Hot tubs, 57
Hydralazine, 64
Hydrosalpinx, 10
Hydroxyprogesterone, 62
Hypertension, 34–35, 47, 64
 and estrogen replacement, 15, 20
 and exercise, 84
Hypogonadism, 47, 48
Hysterectomy, 41, 68–70

Identity, sense of, 160
Ileostomy, 79–80
Illness, and sexuality, 29–59, 110–
 11, 150
Imipramine hydrochloride (Tofranil),
 63
Impotence, 24, 26, 44–53
 alcohol and, 65
 diabetes and, 35–36
 drug effects, 34, 62
 fear of, 98–100
 after heart attack, 32

Impotence *(cont.)*
 hypertension and, 34–35
 Parkinson's disease and, 41
 prostate surgery and, 77, 78
 tobacco and, 66
Impotence in the Male, Stekel, 45
Incurable diseases, 59
Inderal (propanolol), 61, 62
Individual psychotherapy, 152
Infections:
 and hysterectomy, 69
 urinary tract, 21, 22–23
 vaginal, 10, 21
INH (isoniazid), 63
Inheritance, children and, 143–44
Inhibited sexual desire, 104
Insomnia, 93
Institutional living, 111–12
Intercourse:
 alternatives, 136
 and ejaculation, 26
 and heart attacks, 29–30
 illness and, 110
 and vaginal changes, 12
Interest in sex, low, 104–5
Intimacy, 161
Intravenous drug use, and AIDS,
 74
Iron, dietary, 90
Ismelin (guanethidine), 62, 64
Isometric exercises, 30–31
Isoniazid (INH, Nydrazid), 63
Itching, vaginal, 11

Jane Brody's Good Food Book, 87
Jane Brody's Nutrition Book, 87
Jogging, 82
Johnson, Virgina, 23–24, 45, 105,
 157
Jolliffe, Norman, 88
Juvenile-onset diabetes, 48

Kegel exercises, 36, 41, 85–86
Kidney stones, 91
Kidney transplants, 42
Kilmen, Peter R., *All About Sex Therapy,* 153
Kinsey, Alfred C., 45, 136
K-Y jelly, 21, 38, 135

Labia, 11
Lactose intolerance, 19
Language of sex, 162–66
Lanoxin (digoxin), 62
Larodopa (levodopa), 61
Lasix (furosemide), 62
Later old age, 4
Laxatives, 89–90
Lazar, Terese, 72
L-dopa, 41
Legal Guide for Lesbian and Gay Couples, Clifford and Curry, 115
Legal planning, premarital, 144–47
Leriche's syndrome, 50
Lesions, in genital area, 57
Leukeran (chlorambucil), 62
Levodopa (Larodopa, Sinemet), 61
Libido, changes in, 61–62
Librium (chlordiazepoxide), 61, 62, 63
Licorice, 61, 62
Life, affirmation of, 161
Life expectancies, 1, 4, 101, 117
Lioresal (baclofen), 61, 62
Lithium (Lithonate), 62
Liver impairment, and estrogen, 13
Living arrangements:
  with children, 128–29
  living together, 129–30
Long, James W., *The Essential Guide to Prescription Drugs,* 67
The Long Life Cookbook, Casale, 88

Long-term use of estrogen, 15, 16, 20
Lo Piccolo, Joseph, 104
Lopressor (metoprolol), 63
Lovemaking, new patterns, 131–39
Lubrication:
  penile, 24
  vaginal, 9–10, 21, 135
Lumbar disc disease, 48
Lumpectomies, 73

Magnesium-calcium supplements, 23
Male hormones, 8, 47–48
Male menopause, 27
Mammograms, 17, 18, 71
MAOIs (mono-amine oxidase inhibitors), 61, 62
Marijuana, 52, 62, 63, 67, 68
Marital problems:
  counseling, 152, 158
  and penile prostheses, 49
Marriage, exploitative, 124
Marriage counselors, 153
Masculinity, 5
Massage, 133
Mastectomy, 70–73
Masters, William, 23–24, 45, 105, 157
Masturbation, 12–13, 43, 136–37
  in childhood, 103
  after heart attack, 30
Matchmakers, 123
Matrimonial swindles, 124–25
Mazindol (Sanorex), 61
Medicaid, and marriage, 130
Medical help for sex problems, 148–51
Medical problems, and sex, 29–59
Medicare, 155
Medications, placement of, 132
  See also Drugs

Medroxyprogesterone (Provera), 61, 62
Mellaril (thioridazine), 62, 63
Men:
  drug effects on sexuality, 61–63
  fear of impotence, 98–100
  heart disease incidence, 29
  physical changes, 23–27
  sexual performance, 5
  single, 125–26
  and vaginal estrogen creams, 16
Menest (esterified estrogen), 20
Menopause, 9
  estrogen treatment, 14, 17–18
  male, 27
Menstruation, cessation of, 9
Mental stimulation, 45
Mesoridazine (Serentil), 62
Methantheline (Banthine), 62
Methotrexate, 62
Methyldopa (Aldomet), 61, 62, 63, 64
Metoclopramide (Reglan), 61
Metoprolol (Lopressor), 63
Micronized 17-B estradiol (Estrace), 20
Middle age, 163, 166
Migrainelike headaches, and estrogen replacement, 13
Milk, spontaneous flow, 61
Milk of magnesia, 89–90
Mills, Katherine H., *All About Sex Therapy,* 153
Minipress (prazosin), 61, 62
Mono-amine oxidase inhibitors (MAOIs), 61, 62
Monogamy, 55
Monounsaturated fats, 89
Morgan, Suzanne, *Coping with Hysterectomy,* 70
Morphine, 66
Multiple sclerosis, 47, 48

Multivitamins, 90
Myleran (busulfan), 63

Narcotics, 66–67
Nardil (phenelzine), 63
National Caucus on the Black Aged, 121
National Council of Senior Citizens, 120
Neckaches, 9
Negative personality traits, 124
Nerve damage to penis, 48
Nerve-sparing surgery, 77
Neurotransmitters, 45
New relationships, 116–30
Niridazole (Ambilhar), 62
Nitrofurantoin (Furadantin), 62
Nitroglycerine, 32, 33–34
Nonprescription medications, 91
  aphrodisiacs, 51–52
Norepinephrine, 52
Norpace (disopyramide), 62
Nutrition, 86–92, 95
Nux vomica, 52
Nydrazid (isoniazid), 63

Obesity, and sex, 135
Ocean cruises, 121
Ogen (piperazine estrone sulfate), 20
Old age, 166
Old person act, 101–2
Oncovin (vincristine), 63
Opiates, 66
Oral-genital sexual activity, 55
Orchidectomy, 78–79
Organic fitness, 82
Organic problems, and penile implants, 49
Orgasm, 11–12
  and hysterectomy, 69

Orgasm *(cont.)*
  impaired, 61
  lack of, 134
  male, 25
Osteoarthritis, 37
Osteoporosis, 13, 14, 19, 39, 90–91
  and exercise, 84
Ovary, prolapsed, 10
Over-the-counter medications, 91
Oxyphenbutazone (Tandearil), 63

Pacemakers, 33
Paffenbarger, Ralph, 84
Pain:
  during intercourse, 40
  in perineal region, 36
  of urination, 58
  in vaginal area, 10
P-aminobenzoate (Potaba), 42
Pantyhose, 21
Papaverine injection, 47, 48
Pap test, 11, 20
Paralysis, after stroke, 35
Parents, remarriage of, 6
  See also Children
Parkinson's disease, 41
Partners, sexual, problems
  between, 5–6, 104–6
Part-time work, 118
Pastoral counseling, 153
Patterson, Fred, 99–100
Pelvic muscles, weakened, 85
Pelvic surgery, 48
Penicillamine, 61
Penicillin, for syphilis, 59
Penile implants, 48–50
Penis:
  discharge from, 58
  disorders of, 63
  stimulation of, 135
Perhexilene (Pexid), 61, 62

Perineal region, pain in, 36
Perineal surgery, 76–77
Peripheral vascular disease, 50
Personal ads, 122
Personal qualities, 5, 123–24
Pexid (perhexilene), 61, 62
Peyronie's disease, 42, 47, 63
Phenelzine (Nardil), 63
Phenothiazines, 61, 63
Phenoxybenzamine (Debenzyline),
  62
Phentolamine (Regitine), 62
Physical causes of impotence, 44–53
Physical changes of age, 8–28
Physical examinations, 81–82
Physical fitness, 81–95
  and heart performance, 30–31
Piperazine estrone sulfate (Ogen),
  20
Pituitary gland, 8
Plastic surgery, 97
Pleasures of sex, 161
Pondimin (fenfluramine), 61, 62
"Poppers", 67
Porphyria, and estrogen, 13, 16
Positions for sex, 135–36
Postmenopausal period, 12–23
  estrogen replacement, 18–19
Potaba (p-aminobenzoate), 42
Potency, male, 24
  after heart attack, 32
  and prostate surgery, 77
  See also Impotence
Prazosin (Minipress), 61, 62
Pednisone (adrenocorticosteroids),
  62
Pregnancy, fear of, 103
Prejudices against older people, 4
Premarin (conjugated estrogen), 13,
  20, 63
Premarital legal planning, 144–47
Premature ejaculation, 106

Premature menopause, 15
and osteoporosis, 19
Prescription drugs, sexual effects,
60–65
Priapism, 63, 67
Privacy:
in institutional living, 111–12
living with children, 128–29
Progestin, 16, 17, 20
Prolapsed ovary, 10
Prolapsed uterus, 11, 69
Propanolol (Inderal), 61, 62, 64
Prostatectomy, 74–78
Prostatitis, chronic, 36–37
Prostheses, penile, 48–50
Proteins, 87
and osteoporosis, 90–91
Protruding abdomen, exercise for,
85
Provera (medroxyprogesterone),
61, 62
Prudent Man's Diet, 88
Psychiatrists, 152
Psychoanalysis, 152
Psychological aspects:
of heart attack, 32
of hysterectomy, 70
of impotence, 45–46
of male menopause, 27
of mastectomy, 71
of prostate surgery, 78
of sex, 2, 12, 98–115
Psychological counseling:
after coronary bypass surgery, 34
in menopause, 9
for sex problems, 152–58
Psychologists, 152–53
Psychosis, 49
Psychotherapists, 152–53
Psychotherapy, 155–57
Public attitudes to late-life sex,
3–4

Public ballrooms, 122
Pulse rate, in sex activity, 30

Racial differences in prostate
problems, 74
Racquetball, 83
Radiotherapy for prostate cancer,
77
Ranitidine (Zantac), 65
Reach to Recovery program, 71–72
Recreation opportunities, 119–20
Rectal cancer surgery, 80
Rectocele, 41
Regitine (phentolamine), 62
Reglan (metoclopramide), 61
Rejection, in new relationship, 127
Relationships, new, 116–30
Relaxation, 105, 133
Religion, and sexual interest, 7
Religious activities, 119–20
Remarriage, 130, 140–47
Renal disease, chronic, 42
Renshaw, D. C., "Sexual Problems
in Stroke Patients", 35
Reserpine (Serpasil, Ser-Ap-Es),
61, 62, 63, 64
Respiratory rate, in sex activity, 30
Rest, 92–94
Retirement, 109–10, 163
Retrograde ejaculation, 64, 78
Retropubic surgery, 76
Retroverted uterus, 10
Reunions, 122
Revascularization, 50
Rheumatoid arthritis, 37–38
Risks:
of estrogen replacement therapy,
10, 14
of penile implants, 50
Role changes, 106–8
Romance, 161

Rupture, 43
Rural areas, social activities, 120

Safer sex, 54–55
Salt, in diet, 89
 and hypertension, 34
Sanguinaria, 52
Sanorex (mazindol), 61
Schiavi, Raul, 104
Schreiner-Engel, Patricia, 104
Sedatives, 19, 66, 67
Self, sense of, 160
Self-centeredness, 164
Self-hatred, in old age, 4
Self-image of old people, 102
Selfishness of children, 144
Self-stimulation. *See* Masturbation
Self-treatment for sex problems,
 105
Seminal fluid, 24–25, 103
Senior centers, 119
Sensate focus, stages of, 105–6
Sensitivity, 163–64
Separation, late-life, 108
Septra (co-trimoxazole), 62
Ser-Ap-Es (reserpine), 61, 62, 63
Serentil (mesoridazine), 62
Serpasil (reserpine), 61, 62, 63
Setting for sex, 131–32
Sex: A User's Manual, 139
Sex organs, surgery of, 68–80
Sex-steroid replacement, 47–48
Sex therapists, 153–55
Sex therapy, 152, 157–58
Sexual activity, 8, 12–13
 and arthritis, 38–39
Sexual desire, male, 26
Sexual fitness, 81–97
Sexual interest, low, 104–5
Sexuality, 1–7
 drug effects, 61–65

Sexuality *(cont.)*
 and illness, 29
 women's views, 134–35
Sexually transmitted diseases, 53–
 59
Shame, sexual, 102–4
Short-term use of estrogen, 15
Sickle cell anemia, 50
 and estrogen replacement, 13
Side effects of drugs, 47, 60, 68
 of estrogen, 13, 16
Siegel, Mary-Ellen, *What Every
 Man Should Know About His
 Prostate,* 74
Sinemet (levodopa), 61
Singles clubs, 122
Single women, 101, 109
 new relationships, 116–30
Sjögren's syndrome, 38
Skating, 83
Skin, thinning of, and estrogen
 replacement, 14
Skin care, 95–97
Slacks, tight, 21
Sleep, 92–94
 erections during, 46
Sleeping pills, 66, 67, 93
Slipped discs, 39
Small towns, social activities, 120
Smoking:
 and estrogen replacement, 13, 15
 and hypertension, 34
 and osteoporosis, 19, 90
 and skin, 96
Social life, to build, 117–26
Social workers, 152–53
Sores in genital area, 57
Sources of help, 148–58
 AIDS information, 55–57
 for homosexuals, 115
 for impotence, 52–53
 after mastectomy, 71–72

Sources of help *(cont.)*
  with nutrition, 87–88
  after ostomies, 79–80
  with sleep problems, 93–94
  in widowhood, 114
Spa fitness centers, 84
Spanish fly, 51, 52
Special interest activities, 119
Spermicides, 55
Sperm production, 26, 62
Spinal cord injury, 48
Spironolactone (Aldactone), 61, 62, 63
Spoiled children, 142–43
Sports, and urinary infections, 22
Stationary bicycle, 83
Stekel, William, *Impotence in the Male,* 45
Stereotypes of older people, 4
Sterility, 24
  alcohol and, 65
  and renal disease, 42
Steroids, 8
Stimulation, sexual, 8
Strangulation of hernia, 43
Stress:
  and arthritis, 39
  after heart attack, 32–33
  and impotence, 99–100
  and menopause, 9
Stress incontinence, 40–41
Stress tests, 31, 83
Stretching exercises, 82
Stroke, 35
  and estrogen replacement, 13
Sugar, natural sources, 87
Sugar diabetes, 35–36, 47
Sugar tolerance, and estrogen replacement, 14
Sulfasalazine (Azulfidine), 62
Sulfonamides, 50
Sulpiride (Equilid), 61

Sun, overexposure, 95
Suprapubic surgery, 76
Surgery, 68–80
  and estrogen replacement, 13
  and impotence, 47
Swimming, 83, 85
Swindles, 124–25
Syphilis, 58–59

Tagamet (cimetidine), 61, 62, 63, 65
Talking about sex, 138–39
Tandearil (oxyphenbutazone), 63
Techniques of sex, 133–36
Tennis, 83
Testicular disorders, 63
Testosterone, 27, 45, 47–48
  decreased, 62, 65
Therapists, 152–57
Thiazide diuretics, 62
Thioridazine (Mellaril), 62, 63
Thorazine (chlorpromazine), 61, 62, 63
Thrombophlebitis, and estrogen replacement, 13, 14
Time for sex, 132–33
Tobacco, 66
  and estrogen replacement, 13
Tofranil (imipramine hydrochloride), 63
Toxic shock syndrome, 41
Tranquilizers, 60–63, 66
Transdermal estradiol skin patch, 20
Transurethral resection (TUR), 76
Trauma:
  and impotence, 47
  to penis, 50
Travel, 121–22
Trazodone (Desyrel), 67
Treadmill stress tests, 34, 83
Trecator-SC (ethionamide), 62, 63

Trichomoniasis, 11
Tricyclic antidepressants (TADs),
    61, 62, 63
Tums, 91
TUR (transurethral resection), 76

Ulcers, and calcium intake, 91
Ultrasound treatment for Peyronie's
    disease, 42
Underclothes, 21
Uniform Premarital Agreement Act,
    145
Urethra, irritation in intercourse,
    11
Urethritis, 40
Urinary retention after intercourse,
    36–37
Urinary tract infections, 11, 22–23
    avoidance of, 21
Urination problems, 22, 58
    and enlarged prostate, 74–75
Uterus:
    prolapsed, 11, 41, 69
    retroverted, 10

Vacations, 120, 133
Vacuum-constriction (V-C) devices,
    50–51
Vagina:
    atrophy of, 10, 12, 13, 16, 20
    bleeding, and estrogen, 13, 14
    changes, and sexual activity,
        12
    discharge from, 58
    dryness of, 9–10
    infections, 10–11
        prevention of, 21
Vaginal creams, estrogen, 16
Vaginal reconstruction, 73
Vaginitis, 10–11

Valium (diazepam), 61, 62
Vascular disease, 28, 47, 48
Venereal disease, 37, 53–59
    fear of, 103
Verapamil, 34
Vibrators, battery-driven, 136
Victorian attitudes to sex, 100–101,
    103
Vincristine (Oncovin), 63
Virilization, 61
Vitamin B$_6$, 23
Vitamin C, 22, 62
Vitamin D, 19
Vitamin E, 52, 91
Vitamin supplements, 90
Voice, lowering of, 61
Volunteer work, 119

Walking, 83
Walsh, Patrick, 77
Warm baths, 39
Washing of genitals, 22
Weight loss, 35, 87–88
*What Every Man Should Know
    About His Prostate,* Greenburger
    and Siegel, 74
Widowhood, 112–14
    new relationships, 116–30
Widow shock, 112–13
Widow to Widow program, 121
Wills, 145–46
    children and, 143–44
Womb. *See* Uterus
Women:
    AIDS victims, 54
    diabetic, 36
    drug effects on sexuality, 61
    fear of sexual dysfunction, 100–101
    heart disease incidence, 29
    and impotence of men, 99
    physical changes, 9–23

Women *(cont.)*
   sexual performance, 5
   single, 125
Work, and new relationships, 118–19
Wrinkles, 96

YAG laser, 76
Yeast infection, 11

Yohimbine, 52
Youth, 166

Zantac (ranitidine), 65
Zinc deficiency:
   and prostate problems, 74
   and sexual function, 48
Zovirax (acyclovir), 58

About the Authors

Robert N. Butler

Dr. Robert N. Butler, a Pulitzer Prize winner, has been Brookdale Professor and chairman of the Gerald and May Ellen Ritter Department of Geriatrics and Adult Development of Mount Sinai Medical Center in New York City since 1982.

As chairman of the first Department of Geriatrics in an American medical school, Dr. Butler is a national leader in improving the quality of life for older people. He came to Mount Sinai from the National Institutes of Health, where he created the National Institute on Aging in 1976 and served as its first director. Under his leadership, the need for federal funding for research in gerontology gained recognition. One of his achievements was the establishment of research programs for the study of Alzheimer's disease.

A prolific writer, he won the Pulitzer Prize in 1976 for his book Why Survive? Being Old in America. *He is a member of the Institute of Medicine of the National Academy of Sciences, is a founding Fellow of the American Geriatrics Society, and has served as a consultant to the United States Senate Special Committee on Aging, the National Institute of Mental Health, Commonwealth Fund, and numerous other organizations.*

Myrna I. Lewis

Myrna I. Lewis is a psychotherapist, social worker, and gerontologist with a special interest in the social and health issues of midlife and older women. She is a full-time member of the faculty of the Mount Sinai School of Medicine in New York City (Department of Community Medicine). She has a part-time private psychotherapy practice in which she specializes in working with men who are presidents of their own companies or chief executive officers. She is also currently a doctoral student in social work at Columbia University.

Ms. Lewis has co-authored two other books with Dr. Robert Butler, Aging and Mental Health: Positive Psychosocial and Biomedical Approaches *and* Midlife Love Life, *as well as a number of professional and popular articles. She makes regular appearances on radio and TV on the subjects of aging and on women's issues and is a frequent lecturer to professional and public groups.*